The Corruption of Food

How to Win Back Your Health

Lesley Robinson

Lesley Robinson

Dedication

I want to dedicate this book to all those who are trying to regain their health. You matter and are worth the work. Once you discover the keys to take back your health, your life will be changed forever.

Acknowledgment

A resounding thank you to all those who assisted me with the writing of this book. First, I want to acknowledge God, who inspired me to help people reach their optimum health. A huge thank you to my amazing husband, Arnold Robinson, who supported me for the months I was committed to researching and writing this book. His patience, love, and assistance were invaluable! Thank you to my children and grandchildren, who were a huge support in asking questions, making recommendations, and encouraging me. Last but not least, I want to thank my clients who, over the years, have encouraged me to write down my nutritional knowledge in a book so that they can keep it with them. Love to you all!

Table of Contents

About the Author

Lesley Robinson is a Canadian nutritionist, medical phytotherapist, and personal trainer who is very passionate about health and wellness. Her approach to health always includes four important elements: nutrition, exercise, stress management, and sleep protocols. She is known for teaching her clients about their bodies and how their food will affect them. Lesley is a firm believer in people taking responsibility for their health.

Lesley has had her journey over the years with health and wellness as she dealt with depression after the death of a child, a weight loss of 85 pounds, and an adult diagnosis of ADHD. Eventually, she became a personal trainer, cardio coach, and long-distance runner. It was through her dedication to exercise that led to her desire to study nutrition. Lesley studied at Pacific Rim College in Victoria, British Columbia. After six years of study, she graduated from the Holistic Nutrition program as well as the Medical Phytotherapy program. She is currently a member of the Canadian Association of Holistic Nutrition Professionals.

Today, Lesley lives with her husband in British Columbia, where she promotes her holistic health business, "Keys 4 Health," enjoys her family, and makes time for crab fishing.

Page Blank Intentionally

Preface
My Journey into Health and Wellness

My obsession with health and wellness began at a young age. I grew up on a beautiful farm in Limoges, Ontario, and both loved and valued the farm life. The fresh air, open spaces, and the smell of horses bring back fond memories.

My two favorite hobbies growing up were vegetable gardening and preserving food with my mother, grandmother, and aunts. Our farm was on a one-mile-long road, and each family member was built side by side. The farm was collectively run by all. We would plant, harvest together, care for livestock, and even pluck chickens as a group.

I enjoyed canning food with my mother during the summer days and then listening to the lids pop and seal at night while we drifted off to sleep. I'll never forget that smell of vinegar and fresh dill! I was taught how to bake bread, make butter, yogurt, ice cream, and more. We lived well, ate clean, and worked hard.

At the age of 13, I discovered cross-country running, and my love of running would continue throughout my life.

I added other activities like roller skating and cycling, but running was a great joy. I used my running time as a form of meditation and deep thinking. It taught me about commitment, perseverance, time management, and goal setting. Running kept me healthy while giving me confidence. I ran through high school, college, and my working years. I was the Forrest Gump of my social group.

In 1988, I was married and thrilled to be pregnant with my first child. However, tragedy struck, and my daughter was delivered stillborn (January 1st, 1989). My world was broken, and I fell into a deep depression. I couldn't work, would barely leave the house, and began isolating. I spent most of my days sitting in her empty nursery or lying in bed. I was depressed and started to overeat. I ate everything I could to kill the pain with food. Food was my only comfort at that time.

In what seemed like a short time, I had put on 85 lbs. My joints hurt, my mind was foggy, and I found myself constantly out of breath. I couldn't stand to see myself in a mirror. My running body was gone, and I didn't recognize the person I had become.

Eventually, with counseling, I began to get my mental health back on track. I got pregnant and had my second child. She was perfect! However, I was still overweight. So, I began trying various methods to lose weight.

I tried following the Canada Food Guide diet with smaller portions (1000 calories a day as per my hospital dietician). That failed miserably; I had constant cravings and was always hungry. Weight Watchers also failed. Jenny Craig failed. I tried the Dr. Bernstein diet and the Cabbage Soup diet. Every diet I tried failed. I was beside myself and felt like I would never get my health back.

One day, I saw Dr. Atkins' Diet Revolution book. I was willing to attempt one last try. I bought the book and followed it as close as I could. I ate fresh meat, eggs, cheese, lots of greens with butter, salads with olive oil, and small amounts of blueberries each day. I ate until I was full. There was no calorie counting, and I was not hungry. By the end of the first month, I had lost eight lbs. My brain fog was gone, and the lingering depression was lifting.

As my energy was returning, I began to feel like exercising again. Slowly, I started running each day. I could only run between light poles, but it was a start. Around the same time, a good friend of mine took me to a weight loss support meeting. Those meetings gave me extra support and accountability.

I stayed dedicated to Atkins, with occasional cheat days where I would have a carb-filled meal with my girls. I was beginning to feel like my old self again. For the first time in a long time, I felt like I was gaining control of my health!

Eighteen months later, I returned to my original goal weight and felt amazing! My running was on par; I was stronger and faster! I continued to stay dedicated to low-carb eating with the occasional cheat meal. I even walked/ran through three other beautiful and successful pregnancies. The weight never came back on. I would fluctuate 8-10 lbs. over the years (especially during menopause), but those 85 lbs. were thankfully never seen again.

By the 2000s, I studied to become a personal trainer, cardio coach, and weightlifting instructor. I would go on to complete marathons, ultras, and an Ironman 70.3. Training for Ironman required a very fine-tuned nutritional plan. This training taught me how vital a nutritional foundation was for sport, health, and longevity. In 2011, I decided to go back to school. I attended Pacific Rim College in British Columbia. There, I majored in both Holistic Nutrition and Medical Phytotherapy, graduating from both in 2017.

As I began my practicum, I saw how our national food system had failed us. The clients I was working with were coming in suffering from food-related illnesses: Type 2 diabetes, NAFLD (non-alcoholic fatty liver disease), insulin resistance, metabolic syndrome, PCOS, and obesity. My clients had been through the medical system and were constantly recommended the Canada Food Guide diet by both doctors and government dietitians. When clients would see no improvements, they were made to feel as if they were non-compliant and that their excess weight or ill health was their fault. They would be given medications with poor nutritional advice and sent home to feel worse. Some were in as much despair as I was when I was at my lowest. It hurt my heart, and I wanted to empower them to change their lives.

I desired to give clients a chance to retake control of their health. They were not negligent, and they were not lazy! They had been trying to follow a food system that was wrong for them. The clients didn't fail; the Canadian Food Guide and health care system failed them. When clients didn't improve, they were then offered pharmaceuticals to correct it. Those pharmaceuticals often cause other health complications.

I began to teach each client about real food, what to eat, and how that food affects their organs, hormones, and mental health.

Clients were losing weight, reversing type 2 diabetes, lowering or coming off medications, and feeling less "brain fog." As I saw them improving, I began to reflect on how nutrition has changed over the last 150 years. I saw what our food had done to us as a nation and those worldwide. The corruption and politicization of our food in Canada and the USA have all but overwhelmed our healthcare systems. In this food monopoly, the only ones benefiting are food companies, pharmaceutical companies, and government agencies.

As a healthcare professional, I want to see people set free from the confusion of food. I want to see people maximize their health and have the longevity they deserve. People perish because of a lack of knowledge, and I want this book to educate you. I want you to be inspired and knowledgeable. It's time for you to participate in this exodus from a corrupt food system. Now, let's get into this!

Introduction
The Corruption of Our Food

Definition of Genesis: "The origin or formation of something."

North America has never been as sick and out of shape as it is today. In 2005, the New England Journal of Medicine published a report titled "Obesity and Longevity." (Obesity and Longetivity, 2005) The report claimed that for the first time in two centuries, the current generation might die before their parents if childhood obesity is left unchecked. That was an alarming statement at the time, but in 2024, we are seeing it come to fruition. Nutritionists and healthcare providers are witnessing an alarming rise in childhood obesity and related diseases.

Currently, in Canada, over 30% of children between the ages of 5 to 17 are obese. Childhood type 2 diabetes, liver disease, heart disease, and cancer (1 in 260) are all on the rise. These diseases were predominantly seen in the older population but are now appearing in children. (McQuillan K, 2024)

Over the last 20 years, our population has added new "food-caused" illnesses. Some of the current conditions we are dealing with are insulin resistance syndrome, metabolic syndrome, non-alcoholic fatty liver disease (NAFLD), and type 3 diabetes (Alzheimer's). It's becoming evident that our ultra-processed food is making us sick. Inactivity has become the new "smoking," and mental health issues have drastically risen. As a society, if we want to change this trajectory, we must go back to where it all started. Let's look at the history of our ancestors over the last 120 years.

Late 1800s to the Early 1900s

At this time in history, most of our ancestors lived off the land. Many would hunt and fish, and most family farms raised their own animals for their protein sources. Settlers grew their fruits, vegetables, and grains during the short growing seasons. They would spend hours planning exactly how much they needed to plant and preserve for winter survival. They always let 10% of their crops go to seed in order to save those seeds for the following year. They were very resourceful.

Families would butcher the animals themselves, meaning there was little processing done; it was farm to table. Most farms had cows or goats, providing fresh milk, butter, cheese, and other dairy products. All food was fresh and homemade, with no additives. Farmers would store dried meat, garden herbs, apples, potatoes, carrots, etc., in cold cellars to be consumed over harsh winters. Food preservation was a necessity if they were to make it over the long winter.

Our great-grandparents ate their fruits and vegetables during the growing season while they were ripe and fresh. The remainder of the fruits and vegetables that could be kept longer were stored in cold storage. Their meat and fish were salted and smoked, and jerky was a protein staple. Farm-grown grains and corn were ground into flour and cornmeal and stored in sacks or barrels for winter (all pesticide and GMO-free). During this period, food was kept in its natural state.

The soil was richer in nutrients, therefore producing more nutrient-dense food. There was also no multi-cropping and no chemicals used that would leach nutrients from the soil. People ate much smaller portions than we do now. The dinner plates in the 1920s and 1930s were much smaller than we currently use. They were working harder and eating less.

Most people were far from general stores. The few sparse general stores in towns carried local produce, living supplies, and farming tools. Most food came from short distances. Within communities' farmers would often barter for food and work together as a community.

Men would hunt and build together, while women would gather to make food, bedding, and clothing. This is important to mention because those community gatherings made people feel supported. This sense of unity further increased mental health.

Once small local churches were built, families began to gather for faith and fellowship. In every community, the church would be the central meeting place for all events, including weddings, funerals, picnics, and fairs. These community gatherings would make the members feel loved, respected, and connected. It would give them a sense of being part of something "bigger than themselves." Most would not have felt the sense of "individualism" and "isolation" we often feel in our society today. This sense of belonging to the community created better mental health.

What about our ancestors' activity levels and lifestyles? Farmers were up with the sun and slept with the moon. Our great-grandparents worked harder during the spring, summer, and fall, using the winter to rest. This meant their circadian rhythms were set directly with nature. This symbiotic balance allowed their bodies and minds to regenerate and heal. However, even during the long winter, they would keep busy. The men would take care of the animals, cut firewood, and hunt and trap. The women and children would cook, clean, and make clothes, quilts, and other necessary items.

Another consideration was the lowered stress levels our ancestors had. They didn't run on the same "hamster wheel" we run on today. Technology had not been invented, so there were fewer distractions. Transportation was only beginning, and only the rich had access to the new "Benz Motor Car (1886)." Families did everything together: "faith, family, and community" was the slogan of the day. People living in communities knew each other, met regularly, and supported each other. So, what does all that have to do with health and longevity?

Psychologists say that feeling loved and supported in a family and a community helps lower stress levels. Low-stress levels lead to lower cortisol levels. Lowered cortisol levels lead to robust immune systems. Stronger immune systems lead to better health. Although our ancestors died younger than we do today, it usually was not from chronic food-related conditions. The deaths back then were mainly from pandemics, infectious diseases, harsh working conditions, farm accidents, and lack of medical intervention.

Pasteurization and Fermentation

In 1862, French Chemist Louis Pasteur discovered pasteurization, microbial fermentation, and vaccinations. These discoveries were vital to increasing our ancestors' health and longevity. The discovery of pasteurization and fermentation would lead to safe food processing and increased food shelf life. Pasteurization would make foods like milk, eggs, juice, and beer safer, last longer, and become more accessible. The fermentation discovery would be equally vital for people to be able to can/preserve their own fruits, vegetables, and meat. This new process allowed people to preserve their foods for much longer periods. Instead of food lasting just over winter, jarred preserved food could last a year or two.

1918 WWI Tin Cans and Ready-Made Meals

WW1 brought about many changes to our food system. These rapid changes included tin cans (designed for front-line soldiers) and ready-made processed foods for the troops. These were all lower-quality and vitamin-deficient foods. Their purpose was to keep the soldiers alive and was never meant for optimum health. The wartime canned foods were supposed to be short-lived, only for the purpose of the war. This food was not initially designed for use in the general population. However, these new developments led to the food processing we still use today.

After the war, these poor-quality, highly processed tinned army foods were abundant. President Herbert Hoover realized the poverty caused by the cost of war was very evident in America. People were hungry. Realizing they had storehouses of extra tinned food, Hoover agreed to sell these products to the general public. The general population began to get used to these quick, easy processed foods. It was simpler to open a can than to actually prepare and cook the food themselves.

Soon, large industrial production plants were built, and they began experimenting with spray drying, evaporation, freeze drying, and chemical preservatives. These techniques would make it easier to package various types of food. This new way of processing food would further increase the shelf life. Instead of food lasting a year or two, processed foods could last two-ten years.

Early 1900s to mid-1950s: Food Changes Continue

The freezing process was perfected, and this led to TV dinners (1953 Swanson's). Convenient they were, healthy they weren't. A pivotal point to the freezing process back then was that all the fiber must first be removed, or the freezing would not work. Various binding agents would then have to be added to the food instead. However, natural fiber is important for our bodies. Our gut biome relies on fiber for gut health, so you can already see the problems that would lie ahead.

Along with these experimental food processes came new ingredients such as trans fats, seed oils, vegetable oils, artificial sweeteners, various types of new sugars, and a variety of food chemicals and dyes. We were at a time of "food experimentation" on the human population. None of this had conclusive testing; people were simply guinea pigs.

These modern conveniences began to spread into the average home. We soon saw the introduction of microwaves, blenders, and other home appliances, making food preparation faster and easier. Quickly to follow was a wide variety of instant foods: cereal, instant cup noodles, packaged cake mixes, and baked goods. These were all using more trans fats, sugar, salt, preservatives, and dyes. It was faster and tastier but far from healthy!

Cars, Smokes, and TV

By the late 1950s, America's population was increasing. WWII ended in 1945, and the soldiers were home and having children. This population explosion led to our beloved "Baby Boomers." Sixty percent of families at that time owned a car, and life was changing fast. The home-cooked meals were slowly beginning to be replaced with more accessible processed foods. A&W and McDonald's restaurant franchises were starting to pop up all over the USA and Canada. None of us knew the outcome of all these new convenient, fast foods. However, we would discover the grim results years later.

It was also around this era that people became obsessed with smoking cigarettes. It was seen to be sophisticated and even encouraged by doctors. Doctors were frequently writing prescriptions for cigarettes, the slogan being: "A pack a day, just what the doctor ordered." Cigarettes were often prescribed for nervous and anxious people. Some obstetricians would even prescribe "Lucky Strike Cigarettes" for pregnant women to ward off nausea.

Although the first US cigarette plant didn't officially open until 1961, cigarette smoking was rampant. In 1954, 45% of people polled smoked cigarettes. Once again, no one realized the health impact that would have.

TV soon entered the picture. By the mid-1950s, most households had their first black and white TV. In the mid-1950s, we began to see these new "convenient additions" to life merging into the perfect storm. The introduction of ultra-processed foods collided with television (which would later contribute to inactivity), and people were smoking (toxins). What could possibly go wrong?

President Eisenhower's Heart Attack

In 1955, America was shocked when President Dwight Eisenhower had a massive heart attack and remained out of commission for seven weeks. As a side note, President Eisenhower smoked 3-4 packs of cigarettes a day, drank a daily average of 20 cups of coffee, and was a scotch drinker. However, his massive heart attack raised great fear in the States. Men over the age of 50 became worried about their health. The American public wanted answers as to how this could happen. Scientists and nutritionists got to work looking for an answer. What caused the President's heart attack?

Sugar Hypothesis vs. Fat Hypothesis (Yudkin vs. Keys)

In July 1961, a paper was published by John Yudkin (British Physiologist and Nutritionist) titled "Prevention of obesity" in the (Royal Society for Public Health) Sage Journal. In this paper, Yudkin directly links sugar to the cause of obesity and cardiovascular disease.

Later, in 1972, Yudkin published a controversial book, "Pure, White and Deadly." In his book, he points out the toxicity of sugar in the human diet. Yudkin predicted that sugar was detrimental to the body and would lead to many health conditions, including obesity, dental decay, and heart disease. As a nutritionist, he was a big proponent of a low-carb, high-fat diet for optimum health.

He argued that dietary fat and saturated fat were harmless. The fact that John Yudkin was on the advisory panel of the British Department of Health and had been promoting this theory since 1957 gave him sound credibility in Great Britain. In short, he suggested sugar would destroy our health. But he would be fiercely challenged by an American-based "diet-lipid-heart disease" hypothesis proposed by Ancel Keys.

Ancel Benjamin Keys, an American physiologist who studied the influence of diet on health, would challenge Yudkin. Keys proposed a hypothesis that by replacing dietary saturated fat with polyunsaturated fat, we could reduce heart disease. This hypothesis was directly opposed to John Yudkin's theory. One might say the food war was on.

Keys had previously released the "Seven Countries Study" in 1958. In the study, he claimed to have examined the diet, lifestyle, and other risk factors for cardiovascular disease across contrasting countries and cultures over a set period. He claimed the study proved that elevated blood cholesterol levels led to heart disease consistently throughout all seven countries. He claimed the countries involved were the U.S.A., Italy, Greece, Yugoslavia, Netherlands, Finland and Japan.

Ancel Keys was known to be a very aggressively "arrogant" man, and he ruthlessly pursued John Yudkin's theory. Keys had a lot of connections and important friends and could argue to death to support his hypothesis. In 1961, he managed to convince the American Heart Association to adopt his hypothesis as a scientific fact. Yudkin was silenced. Soon, the AHA implemented the low fat, high carbohydrate diet and began to use lipid/cholesterol testing as the gold standard to test for heart disease.

Many doctors today still promote the low-fat diet and rely on cholesterol/lipid testing as the only measure for heart disease. Keys' hypothesis, supported by the American Heart Association, would directly affect the Standard American Diet and the Canada Food Guide.

Important to note: Ancel Keys' theory would later be disproven as the records of his original study were found by a family member in 2011. Dr. Robert Frantz would work on scrutinizing Keys' original study data. The records revealed that the study was originally done on a group of 22 countries. However, because the findings did not reveal what Keys was hoping they would, he set out to cherry-pick the seven countries that would best support his hypothesis.

He had been wrong, and North America had been misled. The conclusion to Ancel Keys' hypothesis and the recommended low-fat, high-carbohydrate diet has led us to this pandemic of obesity, type 2 diabetes, heart disease, and cancer. Epic fail.

Low Fat/High Carb Diet 1977 to 2000s

The sugar and corn producers saw a cash cow once the American Heart Association began following the Keys theory. When you take the fat out of food, it loses flavor. So, step one in low-fat production was to remove fat and insert sugar or high fructose corn syrup. If the public could be convinced that fat was bad and sugar was good, the public would buy into this new way of eating.

The key beneficiaries would be both the sugar and corn industries. Always follow the money trail. The new guidelines of the AHA would soon begin to influence many other countries. Canada included. We will take a deeper look at these concepts in other chapters. At this point, it's safe to say trouble was on the rise. We were eating utterly contrary to the food of our ancestors. Most of our diet was carbohydrate-based, and most of that was ultra-processed.

The low-fat, high-carb diet that was pushed onto North Americans made us sick. In some cases, it was deadly sick. Obesity has tripled since the 1960s, heart disease has doubled, type 2 diabetes is at alarming proportions, and our health has never been worse. The low-fat, high-carb diet was a disaster of epic proportions. As the 2005 article in the New England Journal warned us, if we don't take childhood obesity seriously, this generation will pass away before their parents.

We continue to be concerned about the nutritional value of our current food system. The new ultra-processed foods are almost entirely void of vitamins and minerals. The added trans-fat, sugar, and poor-quality oils make the calories high and nutritional value nonexistent. People feel full, but most are vitamin deficient in one way or another. Concerns about the excess sugar and high fructose corn syrup are real. The long-term health consequences are becoming a hot topic in health circles. The Canada Food Guide and the Standard American Diet continue to cater to lobbyists as well as food producers. It's an actual conflict of interest. It would seem as if we are in a real mess health-wise, but there is much hope!

What can we do today as a society to fix our health? As a nutritionist, I can safely say there's a lot we can do. We can begin by taking responsibility for our own health, becoming informed, and making the necessary dietary and lifestyle changes. You have the power to change your health! Knowledge is power, and I am writing this book to empower you personally. When one family member takes charge of their own health, it will impact the whole family. The following chapters will lead you to your exodus, allowing you to get out of a corrupt and unhealthy food system and into optimum health!

Chapter 1
The Quality of Your Food Matters

"Eat it if it grows in the ground, on a plant or tree, is fresh animal protein, or wild fish and game."

I believe the key factor to the quality of our food is keeping it as whole, fresh, and local as possible. You've heard the adage "garbage in, garbage out." I can't stress this enough, if the quality of your food is compromised and nutrient deficient, your body and brain will also be nutrient deficient! Vitamin and mineral deficiencies lead to dis-ease. There are so many variables as to whether your food is of good quality or not. Let's discuss some of the most important considerations when choosing the food to fuel your body and mind.

1. Eat it if it grows in the ground.
2. Eat it if it is organic (preferably grass-fed) animal protein/products, wild fish, and game.
3. Eat it if it is locally produced within 100 miles or at least grown in your own country.
4. Eat fresh fruits and vegetables while in season.

As a society, we have been trained to run to major grocers for all our food. Of course, it's fast, convenient, and takes little effort on our part. Grocery stores can be quite workable, especially if your grocery store sells fresh local fruit, vegetables, and meats. The problem is that many of the big-name stores are taking over our locally run markets.

These major grocers are selling foods from all over the world. Fruits are picked before they are ripened and shipped thousands of miles away, which causes many quality issues. Instead, the grocery stores should be predominantly focused on selling locally grown, seasonal produce to support our community.

Consider this: most grocery stores in North America are driven by a handful of major food companies. These would be Lowes Foods, Loblaw Company Ltd, Metro, Save on Foods, Sobeys (Empire Company Ltd.), Costco, and Walmart. These large corporations create a food monopoly that works against local farmers. So, why don’t large grocers want to sell local farm produce and meats? The simple answer is that they want bigger suppliers and cheaper food. The worst part is that they don’t care where they get it from.

They are not looking out for our optimum health. They answer to stakeholders, and it is all profit-driven. This is where you get into industrial food producers that sell unethical industrial-farmed meat, industrial-farmed chicken, farmed salmon, and genetically modified and chemically sprayed produce. This can't compare to the quality of the farmer who grows fresh produce and ethically raised animal protein for their own community.

Grocers want large-sized, perfect-looking fruits and vegetables, but everything that does not meet that expectation is thrown out and wasted. They are looking for cheap produce, and the food quality gets lost in the shuffle. Their bottom line is: 1) how cheap can we buy it and 2) how much can we sell it for? The local farmer just can't meet the mass production quotas.

Local farmers must sell their produce at a slightly higher rate because of overhead, which will lead them to become locked out of the market. Local farmers have better-grown, healthier products but have a difficult time selling them. In my opinion, farmers' markets, local produce stores, and butcher shops are the best choices for your food.

If you must use big-name grocery stores, remember to only shop the perimeter of the store. Avoid packaged and ultra-processed foods. Skip any "quick-convenient" food altogether. Always check your expiry dates and "read labels.". Try to buy food that has traveled under 100 miles when it is possible. If that is not possible, at least purchase food grown within your country. The food that has come farther will not hold the same nutrient value.

The produce picked before ripened will sit on planes and trucks, sometimes for days or weeks, before being sold.

The nutrient value of "faraway" or "global foods" will always be less nutrient-dense than local seasonal food. That is just the truth.

If You Can, Grow Your Own Fruits and Vegetables

Why not try something radical and grow your own food? Growing food in nutrient-dense soil provides incredibly healthy produce. If you are not sure what your soil grade is, purchase a soil testing kit. You can always enrich the soil as needed by adding eggshells for calcium, chicken manure for nitrogen, and compost for a natural fertilizer. If planting in larger areas, rotate your crops regularly and give parts of your land a one-season break. Replenish your soil with red clover for places where you grow corn or grains. Remember to companion plant. Some plants help each other to grow (ex: Tomatoes and Basil).

What if you don't have a garden area? You don't need a huge garden space. You can wall plant, plant in pots, or plant in burlap bags. You can be creative. We have planted all our herbs and vegetables in burlap sacks and huge pots for the last five years. The produce grew fabulously, and it gave us a sense of accomplishment. If you feel gardening is overwhelming, start small and use YouTube. In our age of technology, you can learn almost everything about growing food online!

Community-shared vegetable gardens are becoming very popular. Check your area for local gardens. You can rent your own garden space or share one with another family. Some spots even allow you to "work" for your garden space instead of paying for your spot. Eat all your food fresh during that season. If you plan on preserving or canning many jars of produce, I would work out a deal with your local farmer. I would often preserve dozens of jars of tomatoes, and I just couldn't grow that much, so I would ask my local farmer for crates of tomatoes at a discount price.

They would always agree and often add excess vegetables they had at no charge just so it wouldn't go to waste. Our local farmer had so many extra zucchini and squash that I had to freeze much of it one year. It was too much for our family of six to eat. Then, I learned that if you want to eat fresh fruits and vegetables, make friends with your farmer or producer. Once you work out a deal with a local grower, they will usually invite you back the following year. I greatly support building relationships with your producers so that you know where your food comes from. This philosophy also builds community.

Some local farms will sell off their excess produce at reduced rates at the end of the season. Check your local social media sites for orchards, fruit farms, or vegetable farmers who need pickers. You may be able to spend a few hours picking, and they will give you a portion of the produce. We did this as a family with local cherry farmers and apple orchards.

Also, look at what grows around you. We harvested roadside plums and wild asparagus. In BC, apples are plentiful, so we would pick bushels. We would preserve the excess apples in apple sauce, jelly, pie filling, and apple cider. This would cut food costs over winter. Fruit growers hate seeing the food they grow go to waste. Some orchards offer people to come and pick the trees bare.

Hormone Free Grass-fed Ethically Sourced Meat, Poultry, and Fish

So, what about animal protein? Once again, look for local, ethical farms. They are out there. Do your homework and phone around. Some farmers will sell you a quarter or half a side of beef. You pay for the butchering and wrapping; they will box it for you. This can provide fresh meat for a fraction of the price of store-bought meat because there is no markup. A freezer is definitely a good investment. Check with your local butcher for a "butcher's box" of meat. They will sell you a 25lb or 50lb box of meat for your freezer. We have done both over the years. My personal favorite freezer boxes are from our local butcher shop, Glenwood Meats, on Vancouver Island. This company prides itself on fresh, high-quality Canadian meats and reasonable pricing.

In Canada, you can get a fishing license for freshwater and/or saltwater fishing and catch your own. You could also look at sharing a fishing charter with others, and your catch usually will work out far cheaper, even with the boat cost. Most charters will also provide a service to clean and preserve your fish (ex: smoked salmon) for a cost. Another angle is approaching First Nation bands to see what wild game or seafood they sell. It is always fresh and cheaper than store-bought. We have done this periodically, and you are helping your local bands financially.

If you enjoy wild game, find a local hunter. We are fortunate enough to have hunters in our social circle. Offer to help pay for their hunting expenses and share in the game. Over the years, we have been given deer, elk, moose, bear, and prairie chicken. This meat is ethically harvested, fresh, and free from hormones. If you don't know any local hunters, try sleuthing and ask around.

Once again, finding excellent food sources may take time upfront, but as you build relationships with your food providers, it's an all-around benefit. We will cover more in the chapter on protein.

Why You Should Support Your Local Farmers (Organic or Not)

Local and Organic Food Pros: Local organic fruits and vegetables are guaranteed not to be grown with GMOs and chemical pesticides. If it is locally organic, the nutrient content is higher because it is picked fresh within your area and hasn't traveled far. Your body will absorb those fresh nutrients more readily.

I also suggest beginning a relationship with your local farmer, organic or not. Talk to them, visit their farm, and see how your food is grown. I firmly believe in supporting our community farmers and only buying locally when possible. Most farmers will give you fantastic deals on fruits and vegetables as you develop a relationship with them.

The Problem with Global Organic Food: The expense of organic food is significantly higher and may be out of reach for those living paycheck to paycheck. Remember, all fruits and vegetables begin to denigrate once the food is picked. So, the farther it travels, the more denigrated the food is (organic or not). Buying local produce in season would be a better choice for freshness.

The global foods must travel via planes, trains, or trucks, which carry an environmental impact. Another drawback of "global organic produce" is that you don't know if it is organic. Various countries have different policies set on what organic means. The organic farms in other countries may not be inspected as frequently as ours are in Canada and the USA.

You also don't know how the farm is managed regarding global foods. What is their land near to, and are the workers treated fairly and respectfully? Another issue with global farming is whether that country sees any financial benefit or whether the profits only benefit the large companies.

For this reason, I will always suggest to clients that they buy local fruit, vegetables, and meat whenever possible (organic or not). Ask your farmer about vegetable or fruit boxes. In many communities, farmers will run boxes of whatever they have picked that week directly to your home for a small cost. It doesn't hurt to ask, and you are guaranteed freshness.

Support your local growers and eat the fruits and vegetables they are growing in season. It is easy to google your closest farmer, contact them, and begin a relationship with them and your food! Farmers love giving people from the community tours. It's time we stopped giving our money to unknown food producers around the world while our local farmers struggle. If it continues on this trajectory, we will lose our community farms. We will then be forced to rely on these big food industries and global foods.

When a Grocery Store is Your Only Option

So, we've talked about local farms being your best choice. However, not everyone has access to local farms or farmers' markets. When you live in urban or metropolitan areas, you must shop for food. It is still possible to make great food choices.

Try finding a smaller grocery store and ask if they carry local produce. Ask them where they get the produce from and how far it has traveled. Inquire about their weekly flyers and what day they put out fresh produce.

If you shop at larger food centers, you can still pick high-quality foods. Regarding your fruits and vegetables, ask the produce manager where the local or Canadian fruits and vegetable sections are. They should carry some Canadian produce. Also, pick your fruit and vegetables from the loose bulk section when possible. Pick out the best and healthiest-looking produce and avoid any packaged items.

I know the pre-made salads are easy to serve, but they are not the healthiest. Once a fruit or vegetable has been cut to be put into a package, the decaying process gets highly accelerated. Cut and packaged fruits and vegetables will have a lower nutrient value. You also want to avoid all the plastic wrap so as to lower your carbon imprint.

Prepare and Cook Real Food at Home

Why I don't recommend buying pre-packaged cut fruits and vegetables. Have you ever taken an apple, peeled it, cut it up, and put it back in the fridge? It is already browning and decaying by the next day because you have removed its outer protective shell. Cutting fruits and vegetables exposes the phytochemicals to the air, which causes them to die quickly. You get the maximum amount of nutrients when you buy whole fruits and vegetables and prepare them as needed. Simply put, prepare real whole food at home as needed.

Take the time to cook at home. Initially, switching from packaged, easy, cooked food to home-cooked food may seem like extra time and energy. However, with some meal planning and prepping, you will slowly get into a flow where it will almost seem effortless.

Many clients say it takes two to three weeks to get into the habit of shopping, meal prepping, and figuring out how to cook whole foods. After that, it just seems to fall into a routine, and your family will reap the health benefits! You will also teach your children the importance of healthy eating and cooking.

My husband and I do once a week meal prep because we are very busy. Saturday morning, we shop and then cook all the lunch and dinner meals that day. We then place them in individual containers organized in our fridge. We practice intermittent fasting, so we don't eat between 8:00 pm and 12:00 pm; this way, we only eat two meals a day. We can easily grab our lunch and dinner containers and water in the morning, and we're off to work. It was a struggle at first to get this system worked out. However, now it runs smoothly and is an efficient way to set up our weekly meals. Try to find what works for you and your family.

Restaurants and Fast Food Drive-Thrus

I would love to say just don't, but we live in a world where that is just not possible. If you go to fast food places, I have a few suggestions for you.

- Completely avoid sugar-filled drinks or juice. Get water or choose a diet drink (use diet drinks very sparingly).
- Ask if it is real butter; if it is margarine, just skip it. We will talk about vegetable oils in another chapter.
- Order a salad; just make sure you use olive oil and vinegar and ask for some avocado or meat to be added. Avoid the bread and croutons with the salad. I have found almost all fast food places will accommodate this.
- Avoid any sauces like BBQ, teriyaki, ketchup, and honey mustard, as these are full of sugar. Full-fat Caesar or Ranch dressing is the better choice; they have more fat and less sugar.
- Veggies are good: Spinach, cauliflower, asparagus, or mushrooms.
- Avoid any breaded meat, chicken, or fish; grilled is a better choice.

- When ordering a sandwich or burger, order bun-free. Have them wrap it in lettuce instead. Most fast-food places already offer this option. Ask for full-fat mayo or mustard; they have less sugar than ketchup.
- Search out pizza places that offer cauliflower pizza crust (many pizza places already offer this option). A second option would be thin crust. Note: Papa Murphy chains even carry crustless pizza as a healthier option.
- When you know you're going to a fast food place, Google the menu and plan ahead of time. This way, you are guaranteed to make a smarter choice than if you are deciding on the spot. Set yourself up for success.

Summary of Chapter 1

Try not to feel overwhelmed at this point thinking about the changes you need to make. I felt confused and overwhelmed when I started to make my food changes. Here is what I did: I took one tiny step at a time. The more you practice these food principles, the easier it will be. Let me break down the steps in this chapter into bite-size pieces. Start slowly, and even if you make one small change a week, you will be amazed at how easy it comes after a couple of months.

- Buy fresh local fruit and vegetables in season (less than 100 miles away or within your country).

- Give gardening a try.
- Buy grass-fed meat, free-range poultry, and wild fish, and invest in a freezer.
- When possible, buy your fruits and vegetables locally from farms or farmers' markets. Get your produce whole and from bulk. Avoid pre-packaged or pre-cut produce or food wrapped in plastic.
- Wash, prepare, and cook your whole foods at home.
- If you are going to eat out or visit a fast food drive-thru, plan what you will order ahead of time.

***Takeaway from Chapter 1*:**

Buy real whole food, prepare real food, cook real food, and eat real food. Eat your food in season when possible, and support your local farmers!

The Quality of Your Food Matters!

Chapter 2
Protein: Best Sources of Animal Protein (Air, Land, and Sea)

"Eat it if it's grass-fed, antibiotic and hormone-free, unprocessed, free-range, or wild."

Do We Need To Consume Animal Protein?

There are minerals and vitamins we can only source from animal protein. One of the main minerals in animal muscles/organs is iron. Iron is an essential mineral and plays a vital role in the body. It's used to make red blood cells. Red blood cells carry oxygen throughout the body. Heme iron (meaning hemoglobin) contributes to your cognitive function, energy metabolism, and the normal formation of red blood cells. Heme iron is also necessary for the proper growth and development of human beings.

Along with the mineral "iron," animal protein contains the following vitamins: Vitamin A (Retinol), B12, Zinc, Carnitine, Carnosine, Creatine, D3, DHA, EPA, and Taurine. However, before we get into what animal protein you should be consuming, let's talk about the difference between heme and non-heme protein. People and product labels love to throw the word "protein" around, not realizing there is a vast difference between plant protein and animal protein.

Definitions Matter

The Merriam-Webster Dictionary defines heme as "a deep red pigment that contains iron and is obtained from hemoglobin" (layman's terms – from animals that bleed). Likewise, according to the Merriam-Webster dictionary, non-heme means "not containing or being iron that is bound in a porphyrin ring like that of heme." Non-heme is sourced from plants, wheat, legumes, nuts, and seeds.

Heme Iron (Iron Porphyrin Complex): This is found only in animal flesh like meat, poultry, and fish. The body easily absorbs it, and it is an essential mineral, meaning our body doesn't naturally make it; we must obtain it daily from food.

Non-heme Iron: Non-heme iron is found in plant foods like whole grains, nuts, seeds, legumes, and leafy greens. Non-heme iron has less of an ability to be absorbed by the body because of its plant-based molecule-to-iron interactions. Some plants and legumes actually have anti-absorption properties. This means that when they are consumed, there are phytochemicals that fight your body's ability to use that iron properly. Two of these phytochemicals would be phytates or phytic acids found in whole grains, cereals, soy corn, and walnuts. When you consume non-heme iron with these phytochemicals, they block your iron absorption. This may contribute to anemia.

To summarize this point, it matters which type of protein you consume. You could eat an eight-ounce of beef liver and three boiled eggs and get your full protein requirement for the day. Compare that to a full plate of vegetables, legumes, and nuts. You would have to eat three times the amount to get the same "grams" of protein that you would from your steak and eggs. Even if the quantity of protein was the same in grams, the quality is not the same. Heme means blood, not plants. That is why those who are vegan/vegetarians frequently require supplementation of B12, iron, and zinc – they are simply not getting it from their diet.

Here are a couple of well-researched studies you may want to research yourself:

In July 2021, a study titled "Meat and Human Health—Current Knowledge and Research Gaps" was published in PubMed Central. This study spoke about the vital importance of meat in the human diet. It also reverberated that there is no direct link between the saturated fat in animal products and the risk of cardiovascular disease or diabetes.

In January 2024, the National Library of Medicine published a paper titled "Dietary Iron" by Fady Moustarah

Sharon F. Daley.

In the paper, they write, *"Iron absorption involves heme iron from animal-based foods and non-heme iron from plant-based foods and supplements. Heme iron, present in meats, poultry, and seafood, is more readily absorbed and has a higher bioavailability than non-heme iron. Once consumed, heme iron is released from ingested proteins in the stomach's acidic environment and the small intestine."* They later talk about the absorption rate. Heme iron from animal products is absorbed 25%, while non-heme iron from plants and legumes is only absorbed 17% or less, depending on the non-heme source and what it is eaten with.

Now that we have covered why I believe we need animal protein, we need to discuss how to access the best sources of heme protein. Let's look at the differences between grass-fed, free-range, hormone/antibiotic-free, ethically grown, farmed, and wild salmon.

Grass-fed and Organic Beef

Let's consider the definitions before discussing grass-fed vs. organic corn/grain-fed beef. Grass-fed beef means the cattle lived their whole life eating grasses or hay once weaned from the mother.

What are the benefits of grass-fed? The benefit of your beef being grass-fed is two-fold.

1. It makes for a happier life for the animal. The animal isn't living in cramped, unpleasant conditions. They are usually outdoors much of the time.

2. Grass-fed beef contains two to six times more Omega-3 fatty acids than grain/corn-fed beef. Omega-3 fatty acids help prevent and treat many diseases by lowering inflammation. Inflammations lead to many issues, such as heart disease, stroke, and a wide variety of autoimmune diseases.

Organic pasture-raised and organic grain-fed beef are both better choices. Organic means the cows ate organic-grown feed and were not subjected to antibiotics or hormones.

As a nutritionist, I would recommend grass-fed due to its higher levels of Omega-3. The grass-fed beef is also much tastier, in my opinion. Organic grain-fed would be my second choice if grass-fed were not available.

Why is Corn-Fed "Factory-Farmed" Meat a Problem?

The living conditions for animals in large factory farms are less than ideal. They are hoarded close together and overfed with grains and corn to fatten them up faster. This heavy grain/corn diet goes against the structure of the cow's digestive system. They can't digest the heavy grain mixture. This often causes an over-acidic digestive system, which leads to liver complications and other health problems. The animals then need to be treated with injectable drugs to control the complications. The confined living situation and overfeeding the animal will stress it out, causing raised cortisol, which increases blood sugar levels and affects the meat.

Free Range Chickens

"Free range" simply means that the farm allows the chickens to walk freely within an area. These areas may be inside free-roaming, outside free-roaming, or both. They are not confined in over-populated cages. The chickens that roam outside are exposed to the sun, producing Vitamin D, which means it will also pass through the eggs and meat. It also ensures that the chickens are happier, which means the cortisol levels are lower. Meat from stressed animals has a lower PH level, lighter color, and is tougher to eat. Stressed chickens also lay fewer eggs and suffer from more parasites and poultry-related diseases.

Egg Yolk Colors Explained

I often hear from clients that they believe the darker the egg yolk, the fresher the egg. However, the color of egg yolks varies depending on what the chickens are fed. Wheat-based chickens tend to have a paler egg yolk color (pale yellow), while chickens fed a diet rich in carotenoids (lutein, zeaxanthin, and B-carotene) will have a deeper, richer orange color.

Hormone-Free/Antibiotic-Free Animal Protein

Ensure your meat and poultry are both hormone-free and antibiotic-free. Canada banned the use of hormones in chicken on March 4th, 1963. All Canadian chickens are now raised free of hormones regardless of where they are farmed or what they are fed. Hormones are also banned in the Canadian dairy sector. Dairy cows are no longer allowed to be given rbST, so our dairy is hormone-free. These standards are the same in Europe but are not valid for other countries.

Hormones are given to animals to increase their size for market. This is done primarily on large factory farms. Meat (dairy and egg) products carrying hormones can affect the consumer's hormones. The growth hormones can have a significant effect on children going through puberty. The consumption of such products will push the child into early puberty. Antibiotics in animals can be a problem. The large industrial meat/poultry/farmed salmon producers often use antibiotics to maintain their produce. These industrially raised animals/poultry/fish are kept in cramped quarters. If one gets ill, it spreads quickly to others, so they are treated with antibiotics. These antibiotics will remain in the meat, and when we consume it, we can develop antibiotic resistance. Our system will build up resistance, and this will cause antibiotics to no longer work when we take them. MRSA (Methicillin-resistant Staphylococcus) is a group of gram-positive bacteria. This group is different from other Staphylococcus aureus, where it will not respond to antibiotics. This can become very dangerous.

The safest bet is to ensure your protein sources are free from both hormones and antibiotics. Think about calling your local farm to ask about meat sources. Farmers' markets may also have some good leads on where you can buy good quality meat. Many butchers/meat shops offer a wide range of hormone/antibiotic-free protein. If you are getting your meat from large grocery stores, read your labels and ask the store butcher about the meat.

Why Does Ethically Raised Animals Matter?

Ethically sourced meat has a direct impact on our health and environment. Animals raised in an ethical way on a sustainable farm create healthy products. Ethically raised animals are fed nutritious diets with less stress, chemicals, and disease exposure. By sourcing your meat from these local farms, consumers will enjoy healthier and tastier meats while, at the same time, supporting ethical farms and the environment. I am a firm believer in the "Farm to Plate" philosophy. Trying to get your food from the local farm to your plate is always the best practice. So, when shopping for meat, think local or at least Canadian-grown.

Wild Salmon over Farmed Salmon

A case for wild-caught salmon: Wild-caught salmon, or any fish in general, refers to fish caught in its natural environment. This can be lakes, rivers, or oceans with no human intervention. Wild-caught salmon is less stressed, more vibrant in color, and has far more flavor. The nutrient level of wild-caught fish is also much higher than farmed fish.

As a nutritionist, I recommend wild over farmed for the Omega 3-6 factor. Wild salmon has a higher ratio of Omega-3 to Omega-6 fatty acids. As a species, humans ingest far more Omega-6 fatty acids (inflammatory) and too few Omega-3 (anti-inflammatory). We need both, but because most people eat a highly inflammatory diet (Omega-6), we should consume more Omega-3 to lower that inflammation. Wild salmon is higher in Omega-3. As you can see, this would be a far healthier choice. This is directly related to their diet. Wild salmon feed off organisms found in their natural environment: insects, invertebrates, plankton, other fish, and shrimp – all healthy sources for salmon.

The problem with farmed salmon: Farmed salmon is relatively new and not wholly regulated yet. There's a lot of human intervention and control. They are raised in large fish farms, which are overcrowded, so there is a greater risk of disease. They are fed a heavy diet of pellet feed containing a blend of grains, plants, and fish meal. The salmon's digestive systems cannot fully digest these pellets. The feed also includes pesticides (Slice or Emamectin Benzoate) to stop the salmon from getting parasites. They are also given antibiotics to treat a variety of bacteria; all these man-made interventions cause the Omega-6 levels to be much higher. Consuming farmed salmon regularly will increase your level of inflammation.

The color and taste are also quite different. The pellets the farmed salmon are fed cause the meat to be grey in color so that they will inject a dye into the fish for coloring. The taste is far milder, and it has an odd orange-pink coloring.

The next time you are at the market, look for the wild-caught salmon sign and avoid farmed salmon. You can also visit your local fish market, find a local fisherman who sells, or catch it yourself. In short, wild salmon (or wild fish in general) is best for your overall health.

Wild Game and Where to Get It

All wild game is obviously "free range." They live and enjoy their natural habitat. Every hunter I know personally prides themselves on being ethical in their hunting practices. Most just want to catch their food and know where it comes from. Hunting also helps the environment by aiding in controlling animal overpopulation. Hunting helps lessen the environmental impact in two ways:

1. by not supporting large industrial meat farms and
2. by not having your meat transported across the country by trucks, which leaves a more significant carbon imprint.

As a family, we occasionally enjoy deer, moose, elk, and even bear. There are many great game cookbooks out there to give you some tasty recipe ideas.

Keep the Fat in Your Meat

My grandmother used to eat the fat we would cut off our steak. She claimed it was the best part of the meat. Years later, as I began to study nutrition, I understood why fat was essential. Did you know that our body absorbs protein with fat more readily? Our First Nations people knew this instinctively. When we eat that fat with our steak or chicken, it helps our body to absorb the nutrients from the protein. Think of meat and fat as best friends. We were told to trim the fat off all meat during the low-fat revolution. They claimed it was fat that made you fat and would lead to heart disease and cancer; thank you, Ancel Keys. Jumping ahead to today, the new research is telling us what we should have already known from our ancestors. Saturated fat/animal fat is not bad for you. Sugar and simple carbs were the problem.

Did you know our bodies require fat to regulate hormones and brain function? As a side note, when North America went on this high-carb, low-fat/no-fat diet, we began seeing a rise in mental issues, dementia, infertility, and menstrual disruptions. We would not figure out until years later that this was caused by removing all the fat from our diet, which would affect both hormones and brain health. I will mention right here that you will also need to be aware of whether your meat has been injected with hormones. When big industrial farmers give animal hormone injections, the hormones are stored in that animal fat. That would be the only fat I would trim off. I would instead add grass-fed butter to that meat for absorption. If you buy low-quality meat, purchase it without fat and add your own fat at home. But if you are buying grass-fed, hormone/antibiotic-free, then eat the fat that it comes with.

Fat is not only required for the absorption of meat but also for the absorption of vegetables. So, leave that skin on your chicken, choose fatty cuts of grass-fed or organic meats, get that regular ground beef, put some grass-fed butter on your cooked vegetables, and put olive oil on your salads.

Why Processed Meat is Not a Good Option

While meat and animal protein are vital for our health, processed meats should be kept to a minimum. You have already seen a theme in this book: keep your food as close to whole and natural as possible. So, when it comes to processed meats, it is just that – "processed." If you are sourcing your animals or buying organic/grass-fed meats to smoke or cure them yourself, that is a better choice. However, when you go to a supermarket and purchase processed meats, a lot has been done to it. It goes through mechanical separation, then fillers and other chemicals are added to preserve the product. Some have food dye added to make it pleasant in color. Processed meats should be consumed very rarely.

Processed meats such as sausage, hot dogs, bacon, and deli meats should only be consumed occasionally (unless they are organic, fresh, and unprocessed from the butchers). If you are buying frozen or ultra-processed meats, they are not the best choice and may carry fillers and carcinogens. Always ask the butcher at your grocery store how things are made. They may carry organic grass-fed beef sausages, pork wieners, and good-quality bacon. Fresh bacon and sausages from the butchers directly are excellent choices!

Preparing Your Meat to Get the Maximum Amount of Iron

Many people in North America are anemic, especially women due to menstruation or post-menopausal women who have difficulty absorbing iron. Part of that may be simply not eating enough animal protein.

Another contributing factor may be the low-fat philosophy of eating animal protein without fat. Another contributing factor for anemia is people who may have medical conditions (IBS, Celiac disease, Crohn's disease, RA, Ulcerative colitis) or be taking pharmaceuticals that deplete our body's ability to absorb heme iron (tetracycline, penicillin, ciprofloxacin, and anti-seizure medications). So, I will give you a few tricks of the trade to improve iron absorption.

1. Add Vitamin C to your meat. Ascorbic acid will draw out the iron and B12 and assist you in absorption. So, add produce like oranges, lemons, lime, bell peppers, tomatoes, spinach, and cabbage to your meat and fish while cooking. This will help draw out the minerals and vitamins from your meat.

2. Keep the fat on. We have already talked about how meat and fat work together.

3. Cook in a cast iron pan. Cooking meat or fish in a cast iron pan will draw out the iron from the pan itself, increasing the iron levels in your meat by up to 16%.

4. You may have to eat a little more. I used to lean more toward the anemic side; however, my markers started to improve when I increased my meat consumption along with fat. Over three months, my ferritin levels and B12 were slightly above where they should be, and I felt fantastic. Now, I eat meat twice a day and in slightly larger portions. Ask your local naturopath to order a vitamin profile test to check for vitamin and mineral deficiencies and get a clear picture of your iron requirements.

Say No to Plant-Based Meat Products (Ex: Beyond Meat)

When I began working on this book, one of my eight beautiful grandchildren asked a brilliant question. Ivy W (age 11) asked me if the plant-based "fake meat" was the same as real meat. I was amazed at how perceptive Ivy was. She couldn't figure out why people would eat "fake meat" when you could eat real meat. I told her I would add this question to the book and give her credit. So here is the answer, Ivy. No, plant-based meat is nowhere near the same quality as animal protein, and I will explain why. First, remember I have repeatedly discussed in this book, eat real food with as little processing as possible and try to source it locally. We also discussed the difference between heme protein (a fish, animal, or bird that bleeds) and non-heme protein (plants, grains, soy, legumes). So, let's compare these products.

The Ingredients of a Beyond Meat Burger vs. An All-Beef (Nothing Added) Burger Patty

Beyond Meat Burger Ingredients: A Beyond Burger is made with water, pea protein, expeller-pressed canola oil, refined coconut oil, rice protein, natural flavors, dried yeast, cocoa butter, and methylcellulose. This burger also contains potato starch, salt, potassium chloride, beet juice color, apple extract, pomegranate concentrate, sunflower lecithin, vinegar, lemon juice concentrate, added vitamins and minerals (zinc sulfate, niacinamide [vitamin B3], pyridoxine hydrochloride [vitamin B6], cyanocobalamin [vitamin B12], and calcium pantothenate). They use beet juice and pomegranate to give the burger meat its red coloring. I will add that nutritionists do not like seeing any food label that has more than five main ingredients, and I always say if you can't pronounce it, you shouldn't eat it. This product may be sensitive to those with specific allergies and will definitely contribute to inflammation in the body.

Natural Grass Fed Ground Beef Burger (no bun or additives)

The two ingredients are beef and fat. Nutritional value

is iron, zinc, selenium, riboflavin, niacin, vitamin B6, vitamin B12, phosphorus, pantothenate, magnesium, and Potassium. A meat allergy is exceptionally rare. It is usually linked to something being added to said meat when it does present. Studies show us that real meat does not increase inflammation. In fact, it is an anti-inflammatory food. With this, I rest my case. Please eat real food, unprocessed, ethically grown and as local as possible.

Shopping For Meat and What to Look For

Protein is vital to our diet, so we always want to choose the best source. When shopping for meat for our family, these are some of the things I look for. At first, it may be a little time-consuming, but it will become easier as you find your place to shop for your regular meat, fish, and chicken.

So here are the seven key questions to ask when buying heme protein:

1. Where was it grown (local Canadian)?
2. Was it grass-fed, organic, free-range, hormone/antibiotic-free, or wild?
3. What is the color of the meat, and does it look fresh?
4. Look for cuts with fat on fresh, regular ground beef.
5. What is the packaging date?
6. What is the expiry date?

7. Is it pure? Check to ensure there are no additives or fillers (especially in pre-made burgers).

Let's talk about where to find good quality meat. Take some time to Google your closest meat shop, local butcher, and grocers with a meat department. Ask about where they get their meat from. Do they have a "locally grown" meat section in the store? Talk to your local butcher shop about purchasing a "butcher's box." They may sell 25 lbs., 50 lbs., or 100 lbs. of beef, pork, chicken, or a combination. You can choose what you would like in it, and it comes wrapped, frozen, and ready for the freezer. These boxes will be a bit more expensive up front but much cheaper than buying your "weekly meat" from the grocery store.

In Canada, Butcher Box Canada sells butcher boxes of grass-fed beef and free-range chicken. Many of these local farm meat delivery businesses are out there; you just need to find them.

Likewise, for fish, you can visit your local seafood store or fisherman's wharf to see what their fresh catch is. We often purchase salmon in season and on sale from our meat store. We'll buy several fresh salmon and freeze them. Watch out for sales, and make sure you buy a freezer. If you enjoy fishing, this gives you a perfect excuse to escape!

Wild game is another excellent protein source. Find hunters within your family or in your community who are willing to share their catch with you. Whether it's a family member or a community member, you can offer to pay a portion of their expenses. You pay for the meat, cut and wrapped. It's fresh and naturally grown. Every year, we get deer meat, sausage, and ground elk from our son-in-law and neighbor. It's a big help with our budget and a healthy protein source for our family.

Summary of Chapter 2

Heme protein from animals differs from non-heme protein from plants, legumes, nuts, and seeds. You need animal protein and fat to build blood and increase your B12 and iron levels. It is essential to source organic/grass-fed/hormone and antibiotic-free protein sources.

Do your investigative work to find your local (or Canadian) protein sources. Make those deep connections with your meat providers. You will soon get into a regular purchasing routine and have the peace of mind of knowing you are feeding your family good quality meat while supporting your community. Now, let's go over what we have learned from this chapter.

- We need animal protein. There is a vast difference between heme iron (blood) and non-heme iron (plants and legumes). Your protein source should be from animals/fish/poultry.

- Buy your meat locally. If this is not possible, at least aim for Canadian meat.
- Your animal protein should be hormone-free and antibiotic-free.
- There is a difference between grass-fed and grain-fed. Eat grass-fed when you can.
- Between pasture-raised and factory-farmed, choose pasture-raised.
- When you can, avoid any animal or fish that is "grain-fed."
- Try to eat free-range poultry over caged poultry from factory farms.
- Try to ensure your animal protein is ethically sourced. Most local farms will have that covered.
- Choose wild salmon over "farmed" salmon.
- Eat the animal fat with your heme protein.
- Avoid processed meats when you can.
- Use citrus and a cast iron pan to help with B12 and iron absorption when cooking your meat.
- Do not eat plant-based meats.
- Wild game is an excellent choice.
- We also learned Lesley loves fishing.

Take Away From Chapter Two: Eat it if it's Canadian (local, if possible), grass-fed, hormone/antibiotic-free, unprocessed, free range, or wild.

Best Sources of Animal Protein (Air, Land, and Sea)

Chapter 3
Fruits & Vegetables: Enjoy Your Vegetables and Add Some Fruit

"Eat your fruits and vegetables, especially if they are fresh, local, and in season!"

In chapter one, we discussed the difference between local and global organic. We also covered the importance of getting to know the farmers growing your food and buying your fruits and vegetables locally (within 100 miles). This chapter will cover *why* we need fruits and vegetables. You need to know how to choose them, the phytonutrients they possess, and how your body absorbs them.

Five Reasons to Eat Local Produce in Season

To begin, let's cover some reasons to eat fresh fruit and vegetables in season:

1. Seasonal food is exceptionally fresh and tasty! All produce should be picked in its "ripened" state. When fruits and vegetables reach that final ripening stage "on the plant," the phytonutrients are at their highest. The nutrients are not fully developed when a fruit or vegetable is picked unripened. On top of that, produce should never travel days or weeks in

trucks, planes, or trains. The quicker you eat your produce once picked, the denser the nutrients are.

2. Fresh fruits and vegetables grown in season receive more direct sunlight. More sun means higher levels of antioxidants, which reduce free radicals and lower your risk for cancer.
3. If you are canning or preserving your fruits and vegetables, it is vital that the product be fresh and ripe! You want to maintain those nutrients to benefit from them over winter. If your fruit was picked unripe in California and then traveled 23,00 km to you in Canada, how much nutrient value do you think it would have left?
4. Fresh local produce will cost less in the season because you are not paying for packaging, transportation, and fuel costs. You also save the environment by not paying for transporting that food's fuel or energy costs.
5. Eating fresh and in season will reduce waste. If you eat only what is in season and is freshly picked, it will last longer in your fridge.

I realize it may be impossible to source your fruits and vegetables locally. However, if you are going to eat global fruits and vegetables, make sure they are organic and from countries closest to yours. The closer the product is, the less distance it travels and the healthier it will be for you. If you are choosing fruits and vegetables from around the world, select from the Clean Fifteen List and avoid the Dirty Dozen.

What is the Dirty Dozen and the Clean Fifteen? The Dirty Dozen is a list of 12 fruits and vegetables that may contain high levels of pesticide residue. Hence, it is best to purchase these organically. The pesticides on these fruits and vegetables may still exist even after being washed and/or peeled. On the other hand, the Clean Fifteen lists the 15 fruits and vegetables least likely to have pesticide residue. You can buy these non-organic.

Clean 15 in 2024

1. Avocados
2. Sweet Corn
3. Pineapples
4. Onions
5. Papayas
6. Sweet Peas
7. Asparagus
8. Honeydew Melons
9. Kiwi
10. Cabbage
11. Mushrooms
12. Mangoes
13. Sweet Potatoes
14. Watermelon
15. Carrots

Dirty 12 in 2024

1. Strawberries
2. Spinach
3. Kale, Collard/Mustard Greens
4. Peaches
5. Pears
6. Nectarines
7. Apples
8. Grapes
9. Bell and Hot Pepper
10. Cherries
11. Blueberries
12. Green beans

It is essential to wash your fruits and vegetables.

Always wash your fruits and vegetables well before eating or preparing. There are three ways you can ensure your produce is washed efficiently.

1. Soak them in cold water and sea salt for 30 minutes.
2. Soak them in cold water with a baking soda mixture. Two cups of water to one tsp of baking soda for 30 minutes.
3. Soak them in cold water and apple cider vinegar. One part ACV to four parts water for 30 minutes.

> This method is best for vegetables and hard-covered fruits.

Note: Along with each method, make sure you also give the fruits and veg a gentle scrub, rinse, and pat dry with a paper towel.

These methods will remove the dirt and most pesticides, making fruits and vegetables safe for consumption.

Eat a wide variety of brightly colored fruits and vegetables!

The color of your fruits and vegetables will tell you something about the phytonutrients they contain.

What are phytonutrients, and why do they matter?

Fruits and vegetables all contain natural compounds; we call these phytonutrients or phytochemicals. These plant components improve human health, help prevent diseases, and keep the body working correctly. In the human body, phytonutrients stimulate enzymes that help the body get rid of toxins, boost the immune system, improve cardiovascular health, stimulate the death of cancer cells, and promote healthy estrogen metabolism.

Phytonutrients in food come in various colors (red, green, yellow, purple, orange). For optimum health, one should eat a variety of vegetables and at least one fruit a day. Pick different colors of fruits and vegetables daily; think of it as eating a rainbow of produce!

So, how can we tell what phytonutrients are in our fruits and vegetables? Simply by the colors.

Orange and Yellow Fruits and Vegetables

These colors of fruits and vegetables are obtained from lutein and zeaxanthin, carotenoids. They contain antioxidants such as vitamins A and C, oranges, mangoes, yellow peppers, lemons, pineapples, and pumpkins. All of these have large amounts of these beneficial phytonutrients.

Note: Bell peppers start green and eventually ripen to yellow, orange, and red. Therefore, the red, orange, and yellow peppers are pricier. Lutein and Zeaxanthin carotenoids are eye-protective (macular degeneration and cataracts). Vitamin C is known for preventing oxidation damage, thus lowering our risk of cancer and boosting immune function.

Green Fruits and Vegetables

Asparagus, lettuce, spinach, broccoli, cabbage, algae, kale, brussels sprouts, green apples, grapes (and any other green-colored fruit and vegetable) have a light to deep green color. The green pigment in these plants is from the phytonutrient chlorophyll. Chlorophyll is the natural compound that helps plants absorb sun energy through photosynthesis. It is known for promoting human health and preventing many diseases. There are two carotenoids found in green foods: lutein and zeaxanthin. These carotenoids act as antioxidants in the human eyes and skin.

Purple and Blue Fruits and Vegetables

Produce like plums, blueberries, raisins, and eggplants have a beautiful bluish-purple tint. The bluish-purple color is caused by phytonutrients known as (flavonoid) Anthocyanins. Plants produce these phytonutrients to protect themselves against insect attacks, ultraviolet light damage, drought stress, and high temperatures. These phytonutrients promote health and prevent diseases. This colorful group contains carotenoids, vitamin C, fiber, and ellagic acid. All these phytonutrients are antioxidants.

Red Fruits and Vegetables

The red-colored fruits and vegetables are caused by the phytonutrient Lycopene, which is part of the carotenoid group. These include tomatoes, red apples, strawberries, beets, cherries, raspberries, watermelons, and pomegranates. Lycopene has been found to reduce the risk of prostate cancer, pancreatic cancer, and stomach cancer. This phytonutrient protects against oxidation damage, so once again, it may lower your cancer risk.

White Fruits and Vegetables

White fruits and vegetables are also essential. These contain the phytonutrients fiber, potassium, and magnesium. The produce in this category includes taro root, potatoes, cauliflower, turnips, parsnips, mushrooms, bananas, garlic, and onions.

Potassium-Filled Fruits and Vegetables

Potassium is an essential mineral that all tissues in the body need. It is an electrolyte that carries an electrical charge that activates various cell and nerve functions. Potassium is a phytonutrient found in many foods but can also be purchased as a supplement. Potassium's primary role in the body is to help maintain normal fluid levels "inside" our cells. Sodium maintains normal fluid levels "outside" of our cells. Potassium allows muscles to contract and support normal blood pressure. People often add minerals to their water to balance their "electrolytes." Electrolytes include potassium, sodium, and calcium. You can source potassium from the following fruits and vegetables: yams, potatoes, squash, spinach, broccoli, greens, avocado, bananas, cantaloupe, oranges, coconut, and tomatoes. Potassium is also found in dairy, yogurt, cashews, almonds, chicken, and salmon.

Sulfur Filled Vegetables

Sulfur is the third most abundant mineral in your body, along with Potassium. It is made up of two amino acids (Methionine and Cysteine). These amino acids are used to make proteins. Both amino acids are present in your skin, hair, and nails and aid in strengthening your tissues and allowing them flexibility. Methionine is an essential amino acid that cannot be synthesized by your body and must be consumed from protein-based sources. Cysteine is a non-essential amino acid that your body synthesizes; hence, you don't need to consume it. However, you need to consume sulfur in forms used to produce this compound. Most of your sulfur is found in animal protein, dairy, nuts, and seeds. Having said that, vegetables can also be a source of sulfur.

"Allium vegetables" are high in various forms of sulfur. These vegetables include garlic, leeks, onions, chives, scallions, and shallots. Sulfur-filled vegetables are highly beneficial for your body; they benefit cardiovascular health, bone health, blood sugar balance, and detoxification.

"Cruciferous vegetables" are also high in dietary sulfur. These include Brussels sprouts, broccoli, cauliflower, cabbage, arugula, kale, and radishes. They provide sulfur in the form of glucosinolates. They are high in fiber and help to reduce the risk of cancer.

"Leafy greens" provide sulfur in the form of Biotin, aka vitamin H. Biotin is involved in forming fatty acids. Intestinal bacteria also produce this lesser-known vitamin. *I will point out that Biotin (Vit H) is best sourced from whole milk, egg yolks, and organ meats.* These will carry a much higher level of Biotin than vegetables. However, this chapter focuses on plant phytonutrients.

Eat your fruit and vegetables—why I say no to juicing.

I will probably ruin some people's day in this next section. As a nutritionist, I am strict with clients about "eating whole foods" and not over-processing them. The more natural, the better. Juicing your fruits and vegetables may seem simpler and time-saving, but it is far from the best choice. Let's look at why.

1) The high-speed blades of the blender or juicer destroy the cells of the product. Vitamin C is easily damaged throughout the juicing and blending process. Approximately 60%-80% of vitamin C is destroyed after simply squeezing it. So, aerating the produce will destroy many of the vitamins. Like I said in the beginning chapter, unprocessed whole foods will always have a higher nutrient content!

2) Juicing/blending also destroys the fiber. That pulp (fiber) feeds your gut microbiome (improves gut health) and regulates blood sugar by slowing the transit time of all that (fructose) sugar hitting your

liver. Eating whole fruits and vegetables with the fiber intact will help fight chronic illnesses like cancer and diabetes. So, when you process your fruit and vegetables, you are throwing out the best part while destroying many of the vitamins and minerals.

3) Juicing and blending fruits and vegetables will increase the sugar level. When you eat a whole apple, you get <u>one</u> serving of fruit, with the fiber intact, and about 3-4 tsp of sugar. Now, if you have an 8-ounce glass of apple juice, you will need four apples, and of course, the pulp will be thrown out, thus increasing the level of sugar. This will produce approximately 7-8 tsp of sugar in that 8-ounce glass of juice.

4) You need far more fruits or vegetables to make a juice or smoothie, so that you might overconsume your fruit. The sugar in these juices may lead to putting on some weight or overloading the liver and pancreas. It also spikes your hormones, insulin, and ghrelin, making you hungry again shortly after you drink it. We will cover these hormones in a later chapter.

5) Chewing is essential! Chewing is the first step in digestion. When you bite into fresh fruits and vegetables, your teeth masticate the food, releasing saliva. Your saliva carries enzymes that break down food. This helps your body absorb the vitamins and minerals from the food naturally. Juicing skips this whole process, and the mixture goes straight to the stomach.

These are only a few reasons I don't recommend juicing or blending, especially for people who are pre-diabetic, diabetic, insulin resistant, have metabolic syndrome, NFLD (non-alcoholic fatty liver disease), or cancer.

Why many of our vegetables should NOT be eaten raw. I constantly hear about this "raw foods" diet. I have also seen many people who are struggling with digestive issues and malabsorption on this diet. So why is it not healthy to eat every vegetable raw? Some vegetables we consume must be cooked to release the phytonutrients in them. Let me give you an example. We all enjoy a good spinach salad, especially with strawberries! Now, let's take a deeper look at the chemical makeup of spinach.

Mature spinach should be cooked to rid it of the oxalic acid. Oxalic acid interferes with the absorption of nutrients like calcium and iron. So, when you eat raw spinach, you are not getting near the calcium and non-heme iron levels as you would otherwise. For example, a cup of cooked spinach contains 245mg of calcium, while raw spinach only has 30mg. This happens because oxalic acid binds with calcium and iron, making them difficult for the body to absorb. With spinach, the cooking process breaks down oxalic acid, allowing the body to absorb higher amounts of vitamins, calcium, iron, and fiber.

Spinach is not the only vegetable that should be cooked to increase its phytonutrient count. Here are some others that may surprise you: tomatoes, carrots, asparagus, potatoes, zucchini, broccoli, cauliflower, brussels sprouts, cabbage, Bok choy, beetroot, peas, corn, beans, kale, turnips, eggplant. If you are looking for optimum health, ensure you get the most out of your vegetables by cooking the ones that should be cooked and enjoying others raw as salads. Have that salad with a variety of soft lettuce, baby spinach, green onions, seeds, berries, sprouts, some olive oil, and balsamic vinegar!

Why did our mothers add butter to our cooked vegetables? Why we should too.

In the book's first part, I cover the whole hypothesis war between Keys' and Yudkin's fat vs. sugar. The research shows that good fats, including saturated/animal fats, are beneficial, not harmful as first suggested. We are also becoming aware that the fat our bodies require helps us absorb the nutrients in animal protein and vegetables!

The fats I recommend for vegetables are as follows: grass-fed salted butter, ghee, coconut oil, extra virgin olive oil, full-fat sour cream, bacon fat for Brussels sprouts, or even a full-fat cheese over steamed broccoli. This way, you will make your body happy with good fats while adequately absorbing the nutrients from your cooked vegetables! We will talk about fats and their importance later in another chapter.

Best low-carb vegetables! You can add many amazing vegetables to your plate for those following a low-carb or keto diet. Just remember to cook the vegetables that need to be cooked and add that good fat to them! Here is my list of the best low-carb (keto) vegetables:

- Kabocha Squash (aka Japanese pumpkin)
- Green Cabbage
- Brussels sprouts
- Kale
- Jicama
- Bell peppers
- Hot peppers
- Arugula
- Lettuce
- Zucchini
- Broccoli
- Cauliflower
- Celery
- Red Cabbage
- Asparagus
- Swiss Chard
- Mushrooms
- Heart of Palm
- Pickles
- Cucumbers
- Bok Choy
- Radishes

When following a low-carb diet, stick to these low-carb vegetables to stay in ketosis.

Best low-carb fruits! You can enjoy fruit on a lower-carb diet. I tell my clients, “One fruit a day.” This can be a small green apple, pear, or ¾ cup of berries. Enjoy your fruits; just don’t overdo it. They have fructose that can kick you out of ketosis. Here is my list of low-carb fruits:

- Avocado
- Olives
- Coconut
- Blackberries
- Blueberries
- Raspberries
- Pear (small)
- Green apple
- Lemon
- Lime

I also recommend putting citrus on your meats to help with absorption, and of course, berries are lovely in fresh salads or full-fat homemade yogurt.

An apple a day keeps the doctor away! We have been pre-conditioned to think we “need” a lot of fruit to improve our health. In fact, the Canadian Food Guide tells us we should have 3-5 servings of fruit a day. For many people, that amount of fructose is far too much. Yes, the sugar (fructose) in fruit is “natural,” but your liver and pancreas still recognize it as sugar. If you are pre-diabetic, diabetic, insulin resistant, have metabolic syndrome or NAFLD, or are simply trying to lose weight, all this fruit is going to be a problem. You are going to spike your insulin and ghrelin hormone levels!

Did you know that 150 years ago, our great-grandparents used to say, "An apple a day keeps the doctor away?" (1913) The original line was first found in 1866 in Wales, "Eat an apple on going to bed and keep the doctor from earning his bread." Our ancestors typically ate one fruit daily as a "treat," and that fruit was always eaten in season (unless they were stored apples). Fast forward to today, and I am seeing people who are diabetic or morbidly obese eating an abundance of fruit (juicing 5-7 portions of fruit) because they are being told it's healthy. This will set them up for failure.

Summary of Chapter 3

Fruits and vegetables are an important part of our human diet, with some exceptions, which we will cover in other chapters. We need a wide variety of colors; when prepared correctly, they can be delicious and nutritious. Let's go over what we covered in this chapter.

1. Eat local fruit and vegetables in season.
2. Avoid the "Dirty Dozen."

3. Eat the "Clean Fifteen."
4. Wash your fruits and vegetables.
5. Eat various colorful fruits and vegetables daily; they contain phytonutrients.
6. Avoid juicing and blending.
7. Some of your vegetables should be cooked.
8. Putting fat on your cooked vegetables will help you absorb the nutrients better.
9. If you are doing low carb or keto, pay attention to what fruits and vegetables you eat. High-carb fruits and vegetables may kick your ketosis, so choose from the low glycemic index.

Takeaway from Chapter 3:

Eat various colorful fruits and vegetables, especially fresh, local, and in season!

Fruits and Vegetables

Chapter 4
Milk and All Things Dairy: A Case for Dairy

"The history of dairy is complicated."

There's a lot of conflict over dairy these days. Today, you can hardly escape the "dairy wars" discussed on food podcasts, documentaries, and books. Recently, I, too, have been inundated with media information on "the toxic harms of dairy" and how "humans were not created to consume ANY dairy." What I find striking about this is that when you *really* investigate this ideology and its "cherry-picked research," you will discover that the vast majority of the anti-dairy movement is being led by vegan propagandists who feel that humans should not be eating any animal products at all. Many of the other non-dairy proponents are environmental propagandists who believe that animals (used for meat, fat, or dairy) are going to destroy all of civilization. Having said that, there are indeed some issues with the dairy we consume today, but it's not all bad news. I can assure you that consuming dairy (if it works well with your digestive system) will not end the world. In fact, dairy can be a superfood for many.

In 2019, the CDC reported that 80% of the world consumed cow's milk/dairy products. Our milk and dairy products have indeed been altered over the years, and that has caused issues with intolerance. We also know that most adults do not have the lactase enzyme to properly break down the lactose in milk. As with all our food sources, I like to go back to how our ancestors used dairy and how it has changed over the years. This will give us a road map of what is happening with today's dairy products and why so many cannot tolerate dairy anymore.

Drinking milk originated when nomads began to settle in one place and became farming people (thousands of years ago). The raising of livestock became vital for their survival. The livestock would provide protein, fat, and dairy. Throughout history, people have consumed milk – not just cow's milk. People from different regions have also drank the milk of other animals, such as goat milk, yak milk (Tibetan Buddhist monks), buffalo milk, and sheep's milk. All in all, we know for sure is that most of our ancestors were consumers of milk/dairy products.

As far back as Egypt (401 AD), milk was a very important commodity, reserved only for the royal family and the wealthy. The Egyptians believed milk was a superfood. During that same period, Western Europe began sourcing its milk from cows and sheep. However, even in Europe then, milk was only for the upper echelon of society. In ancient history, milk was regarded as one of the healthiest foods. Even in the Bible, when referring to the "Promised

Land," God has described it as the land flowing with milk and honey.

It would not be until the 19th century that milk would become an everyday staple in the USA and Europe. It became more readily available for the standard population, including low-income individuals. During that period, milk was only given to babies and young children. Later, it was discovered that the further the milk traveled from the farm, the greater the possibility of bacterial contamination. On the other hand, if the milk went straight from the cow to the cup, there was very little chance of contamination. However, with the transportation of "raw milk," there was a greater potential risk.

As the transportation of raw milk began, the infant mortality rate started to rise. This became a problem until 1862 when French chemist Louis Pasteur invented "pasteurization." The pasteurization of milk made milk consumption safer for humans. By 1895, pasteurization plants began producing local factory-bottled (pasteurized) milk, which the local milkman delivered in glass bottles.

By the 20th century, milk tanks were designed to transport large amounts of milk to plants that would pasteurize the milk, and thus, they began to mass-produce dairy. By 1930, we had moved from glass bottles of milk to cans and plastic-coated milk cartons that would preserve milk for longer and could be distributed farther away. In 1985, government agencies promoted milk and dairy as a staple for healthy living for *all* ages. Remember the slogan, *"Milk, it does the body good!"*

So, when did we begin to see lactose intolerance arise in the human population? Our European ancestors began making cheese thousands of years ago. The adult population could digest cheese, but not everyone could digest raw milk. It seemed the children were more readily able to digest raw milk than adults were. Research would later find that at that time in history, many of our adult ancestors no longer carried the lactase enzyme that allowed them to digest raw milk (lactose), which was sugar-dominant. Even though children (aged 1-6) seemed to carry the gene (lactase enzyme), it appeared to shut off after the age of 5 or 6, leaving adults with a form of "lactose intolerance." Butter and cheese still seem tolerable to adults, which we think is because cheese is naturally fermented and has added salt. Those factors would make it predigested and more accessible without the lactase enzyme. Why? Cheesemaking converts lactose (the sugar found in milk) into lactic acid. This makes it almost lactose-free, especially in cheeses aged over two years or in butter.

Interestingly, around 35% of the global population today (mainly Northern Europe and East Africa) still carry the gene (lactase enzyme) to digest milk throughout adulthood. They can digest milk with no issues. It's a mystery as to why! So, milk "may do a body good, just not everybody!" However, it does appear that in today's world, that gene is still shutting down between 3 and 6 years old, leaving many young adults, and adults in general, lactase non-persistent (lactose intolerant).

Milk was and is still known as a "superfood," but only if you can tolerate it and absorb the nutrients. If you do not carry the lactase enzyme to digest the lactose properly, you may still be able to consume grass-fed butter, ghee, well-aged cheeses, plain full-fat yogurt, and kefir. These are all fermented, so they are very low in lactose. Some people with mild lactose intolerance can even handle goat's milk because it is very low in lactose.

As a nutritionist, I recommend that all my clients who suspect they can't properly digest dairy undergo a lactose intolerance test. It's always best to know facts instead of guessing. I have some clients who can drink raw, goat's, and full-fat grass-fed milk with no problem. Interestingly, they get ill when they consume skim milk, 2% ice-cream, or sweetened yogurts. That is because they have a wheat/grain allergy and are responding to what the cows ate (wheat, chemically treated grain). This is another reason to always choose organic milk and dairy from grass-fed animals unless you raise your own milk cows. Some people may also be reacting to the added sugar from dairy products.

Remember, low-fat dairy is full of sugar. When fat is removed from dairy, companies must add sugar to make it palatable. This can be a real problem.

What are the symptoms of lactose intolerance? Dairy intolerance symptoms usually appear half an hour to two hours after consuming dairy. People who are more sensitive to lactose respond quicker than others. For those with a slight intolerance, it may show up a couple of hours later. The symptoms are typically as follows:

- Gas
- Diarrhea
- Nausea,
- Bloating
- Stomach pain.

Treatment for lactose intolerance is available. For instance, there are lactase tablets you can take before eating or drinking milk products. You can also add lactase drops to milk before you drink it. The lactase breaks down the lactose in foods and drinks, lowering your chances of having lactose intolerance symptoms. You can also just consume the fermented products listed above to avoid nasty symptoms.

Dairy Allergy: A milk allergy differs from intolerance; it is an atypical immune system response to milk and products containing milk. Cow milk is the usual cause of milk allergy, but milk from sheep, goats, buffalo, and other mammals can also cause a reaction. This is an allergic reaction as opposed to an enzyme deficiency. The symptoms of a milk allergy may be mild or severe, such as:

- Wheezing
- Vomiting
- Hives
- Digestive problems.

Apart from these, milk allergies may also cause anaphylaxis, which is a severe, life-threatening reaction. This requires a client to carry an EpiPen. Treatment for milk allergies would be avoiding milk and milk products. On a positive note, many children with milk allergies may eventually grow out of the allergy. Some naturopathic allergy treatments or treatments from allergists can assist with this.

So, we have talked a lot about the history of and problems with dairy. I'm now going to cover what dairy you should be choosing and what the benefits of dairy are. First, look at the difference between raw and pasteurized milk.

Raw Milk (Unpasteurized): In 1991, selling raw cow's milk was deemed illegal in Canada. However, every dairy farmer I know still consumes their raw milk. Most families also make their own dairy products, such as cheese, yogurt, etc., out of raw cow's milk. A growing number of families consume raw milk because of its health benefits.

Apart from being easier to digest, it protects children against further dairy allergies as it is easier to digest. As with all other food we will discuss in this book, the closer a product is to its natural state, the better.

Raw milk from pastured animals is an excellent source of calcium, iron, vitamins A, D, and K, phosphorus, zinc, conjugated linoleic acid (CLA), Omega-3 fatty acids, digestive enzymes, and probiotics. So, raw milk is an excellent product if you live on a dairy farm and can access pasture-raised dairy cows. *Once again, I will stress that raw cow's milk is illegal in Canada unless you are a farm family drinking from your own cows. Selling it, however, is unlawful.*

Pasteurized Milk: Pasteurization involves heating milk to a specific temperature for a certain length of time to kill any harmful organisms that may be present in the raw milk.

During pasteurization, more than 50% of vitamin D is lost. The primary cofactors, enzymes, and proteins that help absorb folate, B12, B6, and iron are also destroyed with pasteurization. It was believed that more people became lactose intolerant after the pasteurization of raw milk came onto the market.

Pasteurization does make milk safer if you are "manufacturing milk." However, for those of us who grew up on family farms, we thrived on raw milk. I can't remember one family member, cousin, or distant cousin who ever had an issue with dairy when it went straight from cow to cup. That's not to say it never happened to farm kids, but lactose intolerance would have been rare back then. As a nutritionist, I will always try to consume foods as close to their natural states as possible.

Full-Fat Dairy: We will cover the importance of fat in your diet in Chapter 5. Having said that, I will cover the reasons I give clients for consuming high-fat dairy versus low-fat.

1. Fat does not make you fat; sugar, simple carbs, and ultra-processed foods do. Full-fat dairy is satiating and will curb your appetite by raising your leptin levels.
2. Your body requires fat. Fat is critical for brain health, regulating hormones, and other important physiological functions. Fat is also an essential nutrient for maintaining normal metabolic health.
3. Your food requires fat. Fat is good for your health and essential for absorbing proteins and vegetables.
4. Full-fat dairy is a whole food. Because fat is such an essential element of flavor, dairy products usually don't taste as good without it. So, manufacturers will replace saturated fat with sugar and other

additives to compensate for the loss of flavor and texture. Research shows that these sugar additives contribute to poor cardiometabolic health. Saturated fats from whole foods are best for your body within moderation.

5. Full-fat dairy is easier for the body to digest if you are not lactose intolerant.

Low Fat Milk and Dairy Products

Full-fat dairy products contain more calories but also have more nutritional value and less sugar. In the 1970s and 1980s, experts believed that by avoiding full-fat dairy, people would lower their rate of diabetes and cardiovascular risks. When people reduce how much fat they consume, it must be replaced by sugar/carbohydrates. This drastically affects your insulin levels, increasing your diabetes risks. Please look at the following studies on the consumption of low-fat dairy instead of full-fat dairy. You can find the citation in the bibliography.

A recent study showed that people who ate the most full-fat dairy had a 69% lower risk of cardiovascular death than those who ate the least.

One study done by the Harvard School of Public Health found that women who ate two or more servings of low-fat dairy foods per day (particularly skim milk and low-fat yogurt) increased their risk of infertility by more than 85%

compared with women who ate less than one serving of low-fat dairy food per week.

Low-fat dairy and dairy products are ultra-processed foods. The fat is removed, and sugar and vitamins are added back in. It is simply not the best choice. You can incorporate full-fat dairy into your diet, and if you are looking to lose weight, just eat less of it.

Best dairy products for those who are lactose sensitive:

My dairy suggestions for those who cannot tolerate lactose are dairy products with fewer digestive difficulties. Here is what I would recommend:

- Full-fat Greek yogurt (plain)
- Kefir
- Ghee
- Butter
- Heavy Cream
- Aged Cheese
- Goat's milk

Best lactose-free alternatives:

For those who cannot manage any dairy at all but still love the flavor/texture of cheese, I would recommend the following:

For milk alternatives, I would strongly suggest "unsweetened" coconut, almond, or cashew milk; all are healthy alternatives with good fats.

For cheese, I would also recommend "cashew cheese." This is a very tasty product and will satisfy your need for cheese. Be cautious when choosing lactose-free cheese and other products, as they often contain higher amounts of sugar and require a lot of processing. Remember to read your labels.

Why avoid soy?

Why do I recommend nut dairy milk (unsweetened almond milk, unsweetened cashew milk) instead of soy milk? There are several problems with soy milk and soy in general, including that 75% of soy is genetically modified. Soy is also estrogenic. This means it can affect hormones and may cause digestion issues. Soy has been linked to bladder cancer, and children who have milk allergies may also have soy allergies.

Cashew milk as an alternative: Cashew milk is creamy and high in vitamin E. It's very high in iron and magnesium, vitamin K, zinc, and copper. Cashew milk is packed with excellent nutrients and is a fantastic alternative.

Almond milk as an alternative: Almonds are an excellent source of vitamin E, which is essential for cell protection against free radical damage. Vitamin E also supports skin and eye health and is a critical factor in supporting cardiovascular health.

Summary of Chapter 4

In this chapter, we discussed both the importance and complications of dairy. We covered its high nutrient value and the importance of adding dairy to our diet. We also briefly went through the history of the origins of our dairy, as well as the difference between the raw milk our ancestors drank and the processed milk most of us consume today. We talked about pasteurization and the industrial manufacturing of milk. I covered why full-fat is always the best option over low-fat or fat-free dairy. I also covered the lactase enzyme, the gene that breaks down lactose, and how that gene shuts off in most of us as we age. This leaves us lactose-sensitive or lactose-intolerant. We spoke about how some may have an actual allergy to lactose and some alternatives for them. I would tell anyone who suspects they can't digest dairy to ask their naturopath or allergist for a sensitivity test so they know where they stand. However, consider why dairy is a vital food group "if you can properly digest it."

1. Dairy contains fat. Fat regulates hormones and other essential physiological functions for brain health.
2. Full-fat dairy leaves you satiated.

3. Nutrients and the fat in dairy increase bone health, are cardiovascular protective, and lessen your risk of type 2 diabetes.
4. Dairy is high in potassium and can help lower blood pressure.
5. Buying local full-fat dairy is a great way to support your local dairy farmers.

Takeaway from Chapter 4:

Dairy is an important food group with many benefits and nutrients. However, some of us may not be able to tolerate it well. Some people with lactose sensitivities may be able to tolerate fermented milk products. For those with dairy allergies, switch to almond or cashew products as a healthy, non-lactose alternative.

Chapter 5
Fat & Oils: The Good, the Bad, and the Ugly

Earlier in the book, we covered Ancel Keys' "fat/lipid" hypothesis and how he warred against the other theory created in London, England, by John Yudkin, who taught the "sugar" hypothesis. Ancel Keys believed saturated fat was the cause of heart disease, while Yudkins' theory was that the consumption of sugar caused inflammation in the body, leading to many diseases, including diabetes and heart disease. The American Heart Association accepted the Keys' hypothesis, which later affected the foundation of the American Standard Diet and the Canadian Food Guide. They made "fat" the villain while giving sugar a pass. Doctors also began performing lipid testing to check for cholesterol (HDL, LDL, and triglycerides). Soon, this test would become the "Gold Standard" testing for heart disease. However, this testing is beginning to come under scrutiny today as cholesterol is not as simple as it was made out to be.

By the 1980s, the high carbohydrate/low-fat diet (or, for some, a no-fat diet) became the "perfect diet" for heart health and diabetes. After all, this was Ancel Keys' theory, wasn't it? In their eyes, you would be in perfect health if you did not eat saturated fat. However, they totally missed the sugar, fructose, and simple carbohydrate components. You spike your insulin levels when you rely heavily on sugar, juiced fruit, grains, and simple carbs. The constant spiking of insulin causes inflammation in the body; we later discover the danger of this. To add insult to injury, they also didn't realize that we need a certain level of fat and cholesterol in our diet in order to maintain our hormones and brain health. Years later, we would learn that the Ancel Keys hypothesis was greatly flawed. Instead, John Yukin's hypothesis is ringing true today.

What have we seen decades after the grand reveal of this high-carb/low-fat diet? Diabetes and prediabetes are at an epidemic level in North America. We also have new food-related diseases that our great-grandparents and grandparents never had to deal with. These include insulin resistance, non-alcoholic fatty liver disease, and metabolic syndrome.

Drug companies have made a considerable amount of money off many new drugs that treat these food-caused illnesses (medications for diabetes and high cholesterol are just two). However, these drugs would not be needed if we ate a proper human diet comprised of whole foods, exercised, lowered our stress, and slept adequately. Interestingly, doctors fail to include diet, exercise, and sleep in their prescriptions! Most doctors will also not recommend a low-carb diet or the removal of sugar and simple carbs from the diet. Why? Sometimes, you must follow the money trail. Here are two examples: Metformin and Statin drugs. In 2022, the Metformin market was estimated to be worth US$268.95 million. With regards to statins, Canadian doctors write more than 12 million prescriptions for statins each year, making them the most prescribed drug in the country. If our people are becoming sicker and the only ones profiting are pharmaceutical companies, something must change. It's time we admit that this high-carb/low-fat diet was a failed social experiment. I believe there is a better way; we must return to eating a whole-food diet, and for many, that would also mean a lower carbohydrate diet. Fat is an essential part of a healthy diet.

This chapter will look candidly at the different fats, the importance of good fats, and the fats you must avoid. Let's get into it!

We Need Cholesterol. First off, we should talk about the cholesterol in food. We have been told that cholesterol in food is bad and will eventually give us a heart attack. WRONG! Our bodies require cholesterol because it is used to build the structure of cell membranes and make hormones like estrogen, testosterone, and adrenal hormones. Cholesterol also increases your metabolism and is vital for your body to produce vitamin D. In fact, cholesterol is so essential that your body makes it via the liver. For the average human, the cholesterol you eat in foods has minimal effect on the lipid results you see on your lab test. In fact, sugar, simple carbs, liver issues, kidney issues, and thyroid issues have a far more significant effect on your raised LDL and triglycerides than the food you eat that contains cholesterol.

Saturated Fat

Saturated fat is a type in which the fatty acid chains have all single bonds. Saturated fats, e.g., butter, lard, tallow, and cheese, stay solid at room temperature. They're found in all animals, fish, and poultry. Here is some recent scientific information based on a 2022 research paper titled *"A short history of saturated fat: the making and unmaking of a scientific consensus,"* in which it was found out that the original research that "demonized fat" was flawed. I will copy and paste the above study summary directly below. I would say read the entire paper, but please read the summary, at least.

Summary: *The idea that saturated fats cause heart disease, called the diet-heart hypothesis, was introduced in the 1950s based on weak, associational evidence. Subsequent clinical trials attempting to substantiate this hypothesis could never establish a causal link. However, these clinical trial data were largely ignored for decades until journalists brought them to light about a decade ago.*

Subsequent reexaminations of this evidence by nutrition experts have now been published in >20 review papers, which have largely concluded that saturated fats have no effect on cardiovascular disease, cardiovascular mortality, or total mortality. The current challenge is for this new consensus on saturated fats to be recognized by policymakers, who, in the United States, have shown marked resistance to the introduction of the new evidence. In the case of the 2020 Dietary Guidelines, experts have been found even to deny their own evidence. The global re-evaluation of saturated fats that has occurred over the past decade implies that caps on these fats are not warranted and should no longer be part of national dietary guidelines. Conflicts of interest and longstanding biases stand in the way of updating dietary policy to reflect the current evidence.

As a nutritionist, I believe a regular diet has room for saturated fats. You can have bacon with your eggs, put grass-fed butter on vegetables, or enjoy cheese. You can even eat the fat on your steak. Add moderate saturated fat as long as it is not from fried or ultra-processed foods. If you are one of the 1 out of 500 people with hypercholesterolemia (familial genetically high cholesterol), keep your saturated fat to a lower amount. Just remember, we do need *some* saturated fat.

Why butter and coconut oil are essential.

Butter and coconut oil contain myristic acid and lauric acid. Both play specific roles in your immune health. A lack of saturated fatty acids in the white blood cells can stop the body's ability to fight against viruses, bacteria, and fungi.

Why should you eat the fat in your meat? Over half the fatty acids found in beef are monounsaturated fatty acids. These are the same fats in extra virgin olive oil and avocados. The saturated fat in beef fat is "stearic acid." It helps in stabilizing our blood cholesterol levels.

What about the saturated fat in cheese? The fats found in cheese contain CLA (conjugated linoleic acid), which lowers inflammation and may be heart-protective. Full-fat dairy (with a lower-carb diet) will also aid in weight loss. Newer studies on full-fat cheese also show a link to lowering blood pressure.

Unsaturated Fat

An unsaturated fat is a fatty acid with at least one double bond within the fatty acid chain. There are two types of unsaturated fat: monosaturated fat and polyunsaturated fat. A fatty acid chain is monounsaturated if it contains one double bond (mono=one) and polyunsaturated if it contains more than one double bond (poly=more than one). Foods that contain unsaturated fats include avocados, avocado oil, olives, olive oil, salmon, mackerel, nuts, and seeds (almonds, cashews, and sesame seeds).

Monosaturated Fat (Oleic Acid)

Monounsaturated fats are fat molecules that have one unsaturated carbon bond in the molecule. Oils that contain monounsaturated fats are usually liquid kept at room temperature but start to turn solid when chilled. Olive oil is a type of oil that contains monounsaturated fats. Monosaturated foods that I would recommend are:

- Olives
- Avocadoes
- Pumpkin seeds
- Sesame seeds
- Almonds
- Cashews
- Nut butters
- Pecans (my personal favorites).

Polyunsaturated Fat (Omega-3 and Omega-6 Fats)

Polyunsaturated fats are essential fatty acids (e.g., Omega-3/Omega-6) that the body needs for brain function and cell growth. Our bodies do not produce essential fatty acids, so we must source them from food. What foods contain polyunsaturated fats? The healthiest polyunsaturated foods are walnuts, organic sunflower seeds, flax seeds, and fish (salmon, mackerel, herring, albacore tuna, and freshwater trout).

Omega-3 is made up of three fatty acids: ALA, EPA, and DHA (alpha-linolenic acid, eicosatetraenoic acid, and docosahexaenoic acid). ALA is mostly found in plant oils such as flaxseed, soybean, and canola oils. DHA and EPA are found in fish and other seafood.

Side note about the ratio of Omega-3 to Omega-6: In our standard North American diet, we consume a lot more Omega-6s in our food than Omega-3s. Omega-6s increase inflammation in our body. While we require some inflammation to repair tissue (e.g., wound healing), we consume too many inflammatory foods, and people carry excess inflammation in their bodies. Chronic inflammation leads to disease. Omega-3 produces an anti-inflammatory response, so I would recommend eating a minimum amount of Omega-6 while increasing your Omega-3s. Keep your ratio to 1-3 (Omega-6 to Omega-3). Foods high in Omega-3 are cold-water fish like salmon, mackerel, herring, and my favorite "albacore tuna." Try to work fish into your diet daily.

Eggs: the perfect blend! Eat organic eggs if you really want an ideal Omega-3 to Omega-6 ratio! The Omega-3 enriched eggs are the best choice. A side note: One of my biggest pet peeves as a nutritionist is to see people eating egg whites and throwing away the egg yolk. It's similar to peeling a banana, throwing away the fruit part, and eating the peel.

Why should you eat the whole egg with the yolk? The yolk of an egg has most of the nutrients. What is in the egg yolk, you ask? The egg yolk contains high levels of vitamins A, D, E, K, B1, B2, B5, B6, B9, and B12. The egg white also has the B vitamins, but you get a heavier density of nutrition from consuming the whole egg. Eating two eggs daily will give your body 30% of the necessary vitamin requirements.

MCT Oil (Medium Chain Triglyceride)

MCT oil is mainly made up of caprylic acid, found in coconut and palm oil.

There are many benefits of MCT oil:

1. MCT oil is more satiating, decreasing your appetite.
2. MCT oil can reduce body weight and waist circumference if used with a whole-food diet
3. MCT oil gives you more energy. It has a shorter chain length; it moves quicker from the gut to the liver and does not need bile to break down.
4. MCT oil burns more fat!
5. Recent research has shown that MCT oil, along with a ketogenic diet, may help manage the following

conditions such as autism, Alzheimer's, and epilepsy.

6. MCT oil contains fatty acids that fight bacterial growth and yeast growth, making it a great choice for SIBO and Candida albican.

My favorite way to get my MCT oil in is to add it to my coffee. It is flavorful and delicious! It gives me a massive boost of energy for my morning workout. It can also be added to your eggs or salad. However, start small, a half tsp a day, and you can build up to one to two teaspoons daily.

The Fats and Oils You Don't Want to Consume

Trans fat is double trouble for your heart health. Trans fat increases LDL and triglycerides and lowers your HDL cholesterol. Trans fats will greatly increase your risk of heart disease and various forms of cancer. What makes trans fats so dangerous? They are made using ultra-processing and refining procedures. Trans fats are found in vegetable and some seed oils, ultra-processed foods, junk food, margarine, fried and battered foods, commercially baked cakes, pies and cookies, frozen pizza, non-dairy creamers, refrigerated dough, and microwave popcorn.

Trans fats cause oxidization in the body. They have been proven so dangerous that they have been banned in Canada, the USA, Latvia, and Slovenia. Read your labels, and don't consume anything with trans fats added to it. The other name that they could be hiding under is partially hydrogenated oil. Always remember, natural, real whole food will not have these! Fry with lard, eat and bake with grass-fed butter, cook your own food, and avoid consuming ultra-processed, packaged, and frozen ready meals.

Seed oils should not be consumed.

Seed oils go through several types of processing involving heat. This provides opportunities for the linoleic acid to break down. The process of extracting oil from the seeds is done using heat and pressure. This involves dewaxing, washing with sodium hydroxide, filtering, bleaching, and deodorizing. The liquid is then placed in a clear bottle where it will sit on store shelves for years. The glass bottle allows sunlight to hit the liquid and further degrade it, thus oxidizing it. It oxidizes even more when you buy the oil and heat it up. Since these are cheap oils, restaurants will purchase them to save money. Most restaurants use the same oil for days, heating it repeatedly. This becomes toxic. That is why we recommend cold-pressed extra virgin olive oil, coconut oil, avocado oil, butter, and ghee. We also suggest lard and tallow to deep fry in. These natural oils/fats are unprocessed and do not break down or oxidize.

Seed oils can cause real issues in the body. They have been linked to high levels of inflammation in the body, metabolic syndrome, diabetes, fatigue issues, dysregulated hormones, autoimmune diseases, heart disease, and various cancers. They are also harder for your liver to process.

What products are made from seed oils? Seed oils are found in processed foods like cookies, cakes, salad dressings, crackers, chips, candy, vegetable puffs, granola bars, and types of nut milk. Food companies will strictly use seed oils because they are cheaper, and the product will last longer because it is highly processed. Food companies are more concerned about the want profit than your health.

Vegetable Oils

Growing research suggests that vegetable oils contribute to health problems, including inflammation and heart disease. Therefore, I would not recommend the consumption of vegetable oil. Keeping with the theme of eating whole foods, unprocessed and as close to nature as possible, let's look at how vegetable oils are made.

Vegetable oils are made by going through a series of processes, including cleaning, processing, solvent extraction, refining, and packaging. Vegetable oil (and products made from this oil) are highly inflammatory due to excessive processing and oxidization.

Here is one example: soybean oil. Large amounts of linoleic acid disrupt the gut microbiome. Soybean oil can increase the growth of invasive E. coli in the gut. Here are some of the key players in vegetable oils:

- Sunflower
- Canola
- Safflower
- Corn
- Peanut
- Cottonseed
- Palm-Kernel
- Soybean.

Summary of Chapter 5

Our bodies need fat and cholesterol to function properly for our hormones and brain. As with every other chapter, we must stay focused on consuming foods that our bodies and organs know how to break down and digest, or we are at risk. To stay healthy, we must eat a whole foods diet, which includes fats. However, we must avoid fats high in Omega 6, avoid seed oils, and avoid vegetable oils. All these are highly refined and oxidized. Instead, choose good fats such as grass bed butter, lard, tallow, and ghee. All of these are as close to the original animal (product) as possible. On your salads and in recipes, you can add olive oil, avocado oil, or coconut oil (MCT oil). Remember, MCT oil is also a lovely additive to your morning coffee.

1. Saturated fat and cholesterol generally have many health benefits and should not be demonized.

2. Butter and coconut oil are great fat sources that contain myristic acid and lauric acid, supporting your immune health.

3. Unsaturated fat contains both monosaturated fats and polyunsaturated. Monosaturated fats are found in olives, avocado nuts, and seeds. Polyunsaturated fats are found in cold-water fish like salmon, mackerel, and tuna.

4. We learned that polyunsaturated fats comprise Omega-3 and Omega-6. Omega-6 is inflammatory, and Omega-3 is anti-inflammatory. We should consume more Omega-3s than 6s because our diets are already high in inflammation.

5. Whole eggs (yolks included) are packed with high levels of vitamins A, D, E, K, B1, B2, B5, B6, B9, and B12. Two eggs daily will give you 30% of your daily vitamin requirement.

6. MCT Oil (Medium Chain Triglyceride) has a long list of health benefits and is beneficial (along with a ketogenic diet) for the treatment of Autism, Alzheimer's, and Epilepsy.

7. Trans-fats are dangerous and should be avoided.

8. Seed oils and vegetable oils should be avoided because they are inflammatory and highly processed. They are oxidized and can contribute to heart disease and cancer.

***Takeaway from Chapter 5*:**

Fat is not bad; research shows saturated fat can be healthy and properly added to your diet. Dietary fat does not play a significant role in the numbers on your lipid panels. Avoid seed and vegetable oils. Use natural fats and avoid trans-fats in ultra-processed food, deep-fried restaurant foods, desserts, chips, candy, and nut milk.

Fat – The Good, the Bad, and the Ugly.

Chapter 6
Wheat, Grains, and Legumes: Avoid Some and Choose Others Wisely

"Why you should avoid some and choose others wisely."

Wheat and the Issue with Gluten

I recently had a conversation with a woman who believed that we should eat abundant wheat and grains because these foods are found in the Bible. I agree that our forefathers in the scriptures ate grains (along with meat, fish, nuts, and fruit). However, the grains we produce today are so genetically modified, chemically compromised, and ultra-processed that they cannot be compared with what our ancestors consumed. If we could go back 2000 years before food corruption happened, I would be a grain eater.

As a child, I loved my mom's freshly baked bread with real butter alongside my meat and vegetables. However, when I eat the grains produced today, I instantly become bloated, suffer brain fog, and my weight begins to creep up rather quickly. This tells me something is amiss. When I was growing up, I did not personally know anyone who was "gluten sensitive" or had "Celiac disease." Today, it has become common.

Many clients are reacting to wheat (gluten especially) and grains, making us ask some hard questions. Let's look at the wheat our ancestors ate years ago and compare it to today's wheat.

The Original Wheat

The original wheat (Einkorn) is not what we consume today. It was vastly different. That wheat cereal you are having in the morning has been processed repeatedly over the years. The modern wheat grain (Dwarf-type) is a genetically modified hybrid of the original healthy whole grain. This Dwarf-type grain is grown worldwide today and makes up about 98% of the wheat consumed by both animals and humans. It is higher in both gluten and starch (starch translates into sugar, which will spike insulin).

Scientists designed dwarf-type wheat to become resistant to pests and fungi. It was also chemically designed to withstand harsh growing conditions and even drought. The scientific alterations were not made to benefit human health but to produce greater crop yields and make more profits for the wheat and grain industries. The downside to all these changes was that they restructured gluten, the natural wheat protein. When we changed the wheat by restructuring gluten, it made wheat a compromised and unhealthy product – an anti-nutrient, so to speak. This led to humans and animals being unable to digest the wheat grain properly.

I would say humans should not consume the wheat we are growing today. Some natural farmers would also say animals should not be digesting it. With highly processed wheat, carbohydrates break down quickly and become like sugar in the body. This raises your inflammation level and insulin levels, making you gain fat, both adipose (under your skin) and visceral (around your organs). Visceral fat causes issues with your vital organ function.

Let me give a sad example in the food world. How do we get "Foie gras"? The duck or goose liver is a savory delicacy in the gourmet world. The rich, buttery taste of Foie gras is caused by purposely overfeeding the duck or goose grains through a pipe to fatten their liver. The goose is held down and force-fed grains it cannot digest; this ruins its liver (the organ detoxifying the body). The liver becomes toxic as the grains convert to sugar, which causes the liver to become fat. When humans eat large portions of wheat and grains, the same thing happens to us. It compromises our liver, and the liver becomes fatty. In nutritionist terms, we call this "Non-Alcoholic Fatty Liver Disease" or NAFLD. We are seeing a stark rise in NAFLD today, even in young people.

As a farmer would tell you, they use a combination of corn, soy, and wheat grain in the finishing stages of animal growth to fatten the animal up before butchering. It is hard on any animal's digestive system and equally challenging on ours.

The most significant factor with wheat grain is that we don't have the appropriate enzymes to break down this new dwarf-type wheat. To make matters worse, 5% of the proteins in this hybrid wheat are "unique," i.e., they are not found in other grains. They have been ultra-processed (created through genetic mutation). This makes modern wheat more toxic. It is no wonder we are seeing more gluten sensitivity, gluten intolerance, and Celiac disease. This wheat is not our ancestors' original Einkorn wheat; it's not even close.

Issues Caused by Gluten

We should talk about the gluten issues arising from this new wheat. What are the critical food-borne issues surrounding wheat/grains? What are the symptoms? What are the treatments?

Gluten Sensitivity: Gluten sensitivity is when your body reacts negatively to eating the protein gluten, which can be found in wheat, rye, and barley grains. Symptoms of gluten sensitivity include skin rash, nausea, stomach cramps, indigestion, vomiting and diarrhea, sinus congestion, and headaches. The treatment for gluten sensitivity is to avoid gluten products.

Gluten Intolerance: Gluten intolerance is when your body cannot digest the protein gluten. Symptoms of gluten intolerance are bloating, gas, and fatigue, and can be like those of gluten sensitivity listed above. Gluten intolerance is also labeled non-celiac gluten sensitivity. The treatment for gluten intolerance is to avoid gluten products.

Wheat Allergy: Wheat allergy is an allergic reaction to foods containing wheat. This happens when your body launches an immune response to wheat. Allergic reactions can be caused by eating wheat and sometimes by inhaling wheat flour. For some people, it can cause an anaphylactic response requiring an EpiPen. The less significant symptoms of wheat allergies are as follows:

- Swelling
- Itching or irritation of the mouth or throat
- Body rash
- Difficulty breathing
- Nasal congestion
- Headache
- Nausea
- Vomiting
- Abdominal cramps and diarrhea.

Avoiding all wheat and wheat products is the primary treatment for wheat allergy. Some may wish to see a naturopath or allergist to see if a possible way to build immunity eventually exists. This can work for some children.

Celiac Disease: Celiac disease is an auto-immune disorder that stems from issues with your small intestines, preventing you from absorbing nutrients. The mucosa lining of the small intestines becomes damaged. This causes inflammation. Inflammation of the small intestine will prevent you from absorbing nutrients and minerals from your food. This is serious as it can leave you nutrient deficient. Gluten is the key trigger for this response. The symptoms of Celiac disease are as follows:

- Constant diarrhea or constipation
- Weight loss
- Gas and bloating
- Pale, foul-smelling bowel movements
- Anemia
- Fatigue
- Tingling or numbness in legs
- Amenorrhea
- Infertility
- Osteoporosis
- Loss of tooth enamel
- Abdominal pain
- Muscle pain
- Bone pain
- Joint pain
- Itchy skin rash.

Currently, the treatment for Celiac disease is lifelong adherence to a strict gluten-free diet. This includes avoiding foods, condiments, and beverages containing protein gluten. Gluten is found in wheat, rye, barley, and “triticale,” a hybrid of wheat and rye.

Alternatives to Wheat Products

What are some great alternatives to wheat products?

Cereal Alternative: Find a grain-free/oat-free granola cereal such as Inno Foods Keto grain-free granola. It is filled with nuts, seeds, and coconut and tastes delicious. It is great with full-fat or unsweetened almond milk. You can also add it to plain, full-fat Greek yogurt or full-fat sour cream (sour cream can be used as a delicious substitute for yogurt) with a few drops of vanilla and some blueberries.

Bread Alternatives: An entire line of bread is made with coconut or almond flour. Carbonaut Bread is one of those brands. Making your bread with almond flour at home is also easy enough.

Pizza Crust: You can make your cauliflower pizza crust or purchase ready-made cauliflower pizza dough from the market.

Crackers: You can make your crackers using almond flour, shredded cheese, salt, pepper, and water. These are fresh and delicious. There are also many low-carb, wheat-free, rice-free, and oat-free crackers out there as well. Keto Natural's almond flour crackers are one of them.

Note: A product from the "Jovial" company makes organic Einkorn Flour. This can be purchased online at Well.ca.

Rice (White Rice, Brown Rice, and How They Differ)

White rice: White rice has removed its bran (the fibrous second layer). The germ part of the grain, which holds essential nutrients like iron and magnesium, is also removed. White rice is basically starch with little nutritional value to it. It is used as a filler to make humans feel full, but it is far from a healthy food choice. White rice would have about the same nutrient value as white bread. Through all the ultra-processing, it is left devoid of nutrients.

Brown Rice: Brown rice has some fiber and nutrients left in it but is full of phytates and lectins (anti-nutrients). These will bind to vitamins and minerals and prevent them from being absorbed properly in your body. Phytates are anti-nutrients that can be found in grains and legumes. Likewise, lectins also bind to minerals like zinc, copper, iron, magnesium, niacin, and calcium, preventing the body from absorbing them. Phytic acid stops pepsin, the enzyme needed to properly break down protein. Phytic acid also stops amylase, the enzyme used to break down sugar. So, phytic acid prevents both nutrient absorption and proper digestion.

Arsenic is found in all rice, but white and brown grain rice carry more. Arsenic is a toxic environmental pollutant found naturally in soil and groundwater. It is primarily found in pesticides and industry-production chemicals. Pesticides that contain arsenic have been widely banned but have remained in our soil from previous years. Some defiant industries still dump products into soil and groundwater, affecting our food supply. The hotter the weather, the more rice plants absorb this toxin through the water in which they are grown. Although arsenic is found in rice worldwide, North America has the highest arsenic levels. Brown rice has more arsenic than white rice. This is because white rice is stripped of the fiber and bran (the bran retains more arsenic). The brown rice will retain higher levels of arsenic, about 154 ppb, while the white rice contains about 92 ppb.

Rice plants soak up more arsenic from the water than other grains. Even if it is ultra-processed, arsenic remains intact in your rice products. These include rice flour, brown rice syrup, rice crackers, baked goods for breakfast, rice cereals, and rice-based baby foods.

Baby Food Caution: I would never recommend giving your baby, toddler, or young child rice cereal, rice flour, rice products, or rice milk. There are far better choices for baby food, homemade being the best. You want to avoid giving a baby/small child anything containing arsenic, even in trace amounts. We will discuss better choices for babies and children in general in chapter 10.

Ways You Can Prepare Your Rice and Lower the Arsenic Levels

If you are preparing rice, there are ways to lower the arsenic level by as much as 80%. They are listed below:

- Soak the rice overnight with some sea salt.
- Rinse three times before cooking.
- Cook your rice with the ratio of 1 cup of rice to 10 cups of water, much like pasta. Let the water come to a full boil, and then add the rice.
- Soaked rice will cook faster, taking about 13-15 minutes.
- Strain the rice well in a colander.
- Fluff it up.

Wild rice gets the gold star! Wild rice is actually a species of grass, not a grain. It's a grass that produces edible seeds resembling rice and is 30 times greater in antioxidants than white or brown rice. In Canada, it grows along freshwater lakes and marshes and is handpicked. This keeps it as close to the natural product as possible. My favorite brand is “Canadian Organic Wild Rice.” Wild rice has a heavy nutrient component, has 30-40% less carbohydrates, has more protein, and is tastier! Wild rice may still have a smaller level of arsenic, depending on where it is picked from. It can be prepared the same way mentioned above, but it needs more cooking time.

My Opinion on Rice: In a perfect world, I would say "no" to all rice unless you need it to survive possible starvation. There are far better choices, like wild rice, a nutrient-dense food that is not ultra-processed. Many of my clients have switched to cauliflower rice. You can make your own by grating cauliflower and cooking it with other vegetables and seasonings. Both are fantastic, healthy alternatives to rice grains.

What About Oats?

Most of our oats today are highly processed; unless organic, they will likely have been grown using pesticides. Oats contain phytic acid, which impairs the absorption of iron, zinc, calcium, and more. It also blocks the production of digestive enzymes. This makes oats harder to digest.

Food companies go to great lengths to promote oats as a healthy breakfast or baking option. However, it impacts our blood sugar levels and, thus, our metabolism. Oatmeal spikes your blood sugar levels quickly, even more, when consumed with dried fruit, fruit, brown sugar, or honey.

This makes a combination that drastically spikes your blood sugar. Those with diabetes, pre-diabetes, insulin resistance, non-alcoholic fatty liver disease, or metabolic syndrome should avoid oats altogether.

Another issue with oats is the issue with glyphosates. Glyphosate is a weed killer (found in Roundup) that has been discovered in industrial-grown oats. Glyphosates cause inflammation and oxidative stress in our cells.

For people who are not overweight, are healthy, and can process oats, I would suggest three options:

Organic Steel-Cut Oats: Steel-cut oats are coarse oats that are the least processed. The processing of steel-cut oats involves chopping whole groats into smaller pieces using steel blades. These oats will take longer to cook, but they are a better option than processed quick oats.

Glyphosate-Free Oatmeal: A new product from Edison Grainery called (Glyphosate-Free Oatmeal) could be an option for some.

Lupini Bean Products: Those who want an oatmeal-type breakfast without the oats can choose hot cereals made with Lupini Flakes. Lupini beans are a great source of manganese, copper, magnesium, phosphorus, potassium, and zinc. The company Aviate makes a hot breakfast cereal from the Lupini bean. Some clients enjoy it with cinnamon, crushed nuts, seeds, and blueberries.

<u>Corn, Corn Products, and Corn Syrup</u>

Indigenous farmers in Mexico began domesticating "teosinte" (the ancient corn) almost 10,000 years ago. This corn originally grew wild. The ancient teosinte plant would produce hundreds of thin, wheat-looking ears with no more than a dozen hard kernels on it. Our domesticated corn (maize) is a 12-inch ear of modern corn that can produce more than 500 soft kernels. Our corn kernels today are softer and more delicate but harder for our bodies to digest.

Below is a diagram that shows the difference between the original corn (Teosinte) and our modern-day corn today.

Today, 88% of our corn in Canada is genetically modified to resist pests and tolerate a variety of herbicides. This common-day corn is very high in starch and can spike blood sugar rapidly. That means it is not suitable for those who are insulin-resistant or are dealing with metabolic syndrome, pre-diabetes, or diabetes. Today's corn products are ultra-processed and lack high nutrient value; they are more of a filler.

Continuing with the theme of this book, whole-natural foods are the best choice and have a higher level of vitamins and nutrients. So, if it is corn season and you are barbequing or growing corn yourself, enjoy that corn on the cob. Have your corn with grass-fed butter and sea salt, and enjoy it. In this section of the "issue with corn," I am directing it toward people consuming high levels of corn products (those on high-carb diets), especially those eating an abundance of ultra-processed foods made with corn flour, corn meal, or high fructose corn syrup. The average person just wants to enjoy fresh corn when it's in season; they should do so!

Highly Processed Corn Products: In the fruit chapter, we discussed how blending or juicing your fruit removes the fiber and raises the sugar content. The same can be said in the process of grinding and processing corn. Maize already has a high starch content (remember, starch breaks down into sugar in your body), so when you process corn, you end up with a very high-sugar product. Maize/corn flour makes tortillas, processed bread, muffins, doughnuts, pancake mixes, infant foods, biscuits, wafers, breakfast cereals, and breading. Corn is also regularly used as a filler, binder, and carrier for processed meats. These are ultra-processed foods that spike blood sugar levels and cause inflammation.

Top Concerns for Those Consuming a High Level of Corn or Corn Products:

1. Corn intolerance or corn allergies (rare, but they do exist).
2. Risk of Pellagra (a deficiency of vitamin B3 - niacin).
3. Raises blood sugar quickly; therefore, it should not be overly consumed by diabetics, those with pre-diabetes, those with insulin resistance, metabolic syndrome, or NAFLD.

4. Causes gastrointestinal issues like gas, bloating, and diarrhea for some.
5. Weight gain if you eat a high-carb diet with many calories from corn or corn products.

High Fructose Corn Syrup should not be consumed, period.

High fructose corn syrup is a sweetener derived from cornstarch. Starch is a chain of glucose (simple sugar) molecules joined together. Corn syrup is 100 percent glucose. It is obtained from the breakdown of cornstarch into individual glucose molecules. When making high fructose corn syrup, enzymes need to be added to corn syrup to change some of the glucose into another simple sugar called fructose. High fructose corn syrup increases your risk of chronic diseases, including obesity, diabetes, NAFLD, insulin resistance, metabolic syndrome, hypertension, and heart disease (arteriosclerosis).

Foods containing high fructose corn syrup include:

- Fast food
- Fruit popsicles
- Juices
- Bread
- Cookies
- Cold cereals
- Candy
- Ketchup

- Lunch meats
- Yogurts
- Soups
- Jams
- Chocolate syrup.

I strongly suggest you read your labels and avoid anything made with HFCS. I imagine this will eventually be banned in North America, just as trans fats were. Some countries have already taken a stand against HFCS, such as India, Ireland, Sweden, Austria, Uruguay, and Lithuania. I am hoping Canada and the USA will be next!

Corn Allergy: Corn allergies are less common than wheat, dairy, nuts, and shellfish, but they still exist. People who are allergic to corn don't always react the same way. Typical reactions include:

- Hives
- Skin rash
- Eczema
- Abdominal pain
- Sinus issues
- Sneezing
- Asthma
- Trouble breathing.

However, a rare few suffer from anaphylactic reactions, which are life-threatening and will require an EpiPen for safety. As you can see, the symptoms can range widely.

Currently, the treatment for corn allergy is the removal and avoidance of all corn products from the diet.

Legumes: Legumes are plants in the Fabaceae family that contain a fruit/seed. The produce from these grains is a dried seed/fruit consumed by humans and animals. Legumes are also known as pulses. These include beans (lima/kidney/butter), soybeans, chickpeas, peanuts, lentils, lupins, peas, carob, etc. Legumes contain fiber, non-heme (plant) protein, carbohydrates, B vitamins, iron, copper, magnesium, manganese, zinc, and phosphorous.

The Downside of Legumes: Along with some excellent nutrient content, legumes also carry lectin. What is lectin? Lectin is known as an anti-nutrient. It is a protein that binds to specific carbohydrates. Almost all our plant and animal-based food has some level of lectin, but legumes carry the highest amount. What is the effect of consuming too many legumes?

A diet high in legumes could be a problem, especially in three areas:

1. **Damage to Your Digestive System:** Some specific lectins may bind to the walls of your digestive system. For some people, this will lead to some gastrointestinal issues. Phytohemagglutinin can cause abdominal pain, vomiting, and diarrhea. A female client I had years ago (age 30) was suffering a plethora of gastrointestinal issues and chronic

diarrhea. She also had acne on her forehead, suffered from hair loss, and had constant brain fog. She was vegetarian as per her culture (Punjabi/India); thus, most of her diet consisted of carbohydrates, legumes (Dahl), and sugar. She had not had a normal solid bowel movement for years. She was morbidly obese and pre-diabetic. We eventually found out she was reacting to both the legumes and sugar through an investigation of her diet. Although she was overweight, she had many vitamin deficiencies and was quite unwell. After changing her diet and removing the key instigators (all sugar and all legumes), she began to lose weight and improve her markers.

2. **Malnourishment**: Certain types of lectins also prevent your body from absorbing vitamins and nutrients. In some individuals, the long-term high consumption of legumes can cause malnourishment (vitamin and mineral deficiencies).

3. **Possible Cause of Autoimmune Disorders:** There is currently some new research being done to determine whether lectins can cause symptoms of auto-immune disorders. However, nothing has proven this yet.

4. **Acute Lectin Poisoning:** Symptoms of acute lectin poisoning include nausea, vomiting, and diarrhea.

Can some people still consume legumes? The short answer is yes. We know that you can cut down much of the lectin by soaking your beans overnight, rinsing repeatedly, and then boiling them for 10-15 minutes. Having said that,

I am not a big fan of legumes. People who are struggling with excess weight or health issues like NFLD, metabolic syndrome, diabetes, pre-diabetes, autoimmune disorders, or insulin resistance should avoid legumes altogether.

If you are healthy and do not react to legumes, enjoy them as a side dish. Make sure they are prepared properly to ensure the lectin is mostly removed. I would still avoid eating large portions of legumes.

Summary of Chapter 6

In this chapter, we learned that the grains and corn we consume are different from our ancestors. There has been so much genetic modification and processing done to these foods they are almost unrecognizable. They offer more harm to the human body than good. We learned about the arsenic in rice and that wild rice has less. We talked about corn and the problem with high fructose corn syrup. I covered the topic of legumes; they carry the protein lectin that can wreak havoc with our bodies. These should be avoided unless you are in good health. If you eat them, prepare them properly and consume them in small amounts.

1. The wheat we consume today is grossly adulterated unless you are growing it organically, milling it yourself, and preparing it yourself. There are also companies out there selling original wheat, such as "Organic Einkorn Flour."

2. Some people have wheat allergies and sensitivities.

3. Gluten is a very real problem for some (gluten intolerance, sensitives, and celiac disease are all results of our poor quality "new wheat").

4. Oats are a highly processed product today. Oats spike insulin levels; they are a poor option for those who struggle with weight, inflammation, NAFLD, insulin resistance, metabolic syndrome, or diabetes. Oats may also contain glyphosates (a weed killer). We discussed the alternate options for oats: organic steel-cut oats, glyphosate-free oats, or lupin flakes.

5. White and brown rice products contain very little nutritional value and contain levels of arsenic (brown rice carries more arsenic). Rice needs to be prepared carefully. Rice products should never be fed to babies, toddlers, or children. Wild rice (grass, not grain) can be a great alternative to brown or white rice, but it must still be prepared like the other rice.

6. Corn today is genetically altered; the corn products are considered ultra-processed. This leaves them full of starch and devoid of nutrients. I suggest avoiding corn flour, corn meal, corn oil, and corn products if you have underlying health concerns. Stick with eating corn on the cob in season and skip the processed products

7. Legumes are a toss-up. They do have nutritional value; however, they contain high levels of lectin. Lectin is a protein that binds to carbohydrates and is considered an anti-nutrient. There are ways of

preparing legumes to lessen the lectin. The only people who should consume legumes are those who are healthy and have no preconditions. They should ensure they prepare the legumes properly and eat them in small amounts.

Takeaway from Chapter 6:

The grains, oats, and corn we eat today are not the same ones our ancestors consumed. They are causing health issues our great-grandparents would never have had to deal with 150 years ago. Perhaps skip the grains, eat fresh corn in season, and be very cautious with your legumes.

Wheat, Grains, and Legumes

Chapter 7
Nuts & Seeds: Flavorful Treats Full of Nutrition

Nuts and seeds are the best snacks to top up our nutritional needs! Not only are they delicious, but they're also loaded with nutrients and an excellent source of healthy fats. Nuts and seeds can and should be added to any diet as long as there are no nut or seed allergies.

Nuts and seeds are an excellent non-heme (plant) protein source. They contain healthy fats, fiber, and an assortment of both vitamins and minerals. They can help maintain body weight because their fats are not entirely absorbed. Both nuts and seeds contain unsaturated fats and other vital nutrients that protect against heart disease and diabetes. Every nut has a similar macronutrient profile of protein, carbohydrates, and fats. Different varieties of nuts may have slightly different vitamin and mineral content, which we will cover in this chapter.

Nuts

Why are nuts important? Nuts are rich in phytonutrients that act as antioxidants and contain vitamins and minerals, including vitamin E, B6, niacin and folate, magnesium, zinc, plant iron, calcium, copper, selenium, phosphorus, and potassium. So, your little snack is launching your body and mind into optimum health!

I recommend a small handful of nuts and seeds a day. These can be added to your food or as a mid-day/evening snack. When included as a snack while following a lower-carb whole-food diet, nuts have been known to speed up weight loss, thus improving heart health and lowering your risk of diabetes, obesity, and NAFLD. Nuts and seeds are satiating, so they will decrease your hunger.

Let's look at the various nut types and what they offer.

Almonds: Almonds contain good fats (80% monounsaturated, 15% polyunsaturated, and 5% saturated). They are a great source of vitamin E, magnesium, copper, and antioxidants. They carry many health benefits because of their phytonutrients. Almonds are a staple for low-carb diets. Almond flour can be used instead of flour to make bread, pastries, and baked goods.

Brazil Nuts: Brazil nuts also fit into a low-carb diet. They are an excellent source of calcium, potassium, magnesium, and selenium. However, Brazil nuts contain more than the recommended daily selenium intake (55 mg). Caution: One ounce of Brazil nuts provides 543 mg of selenium, over the recommended limit (400 grams). So, enjoy them, but don't overdo it. I suggest mixing them in with some other nuts and seeds.

Cashew Nuts: Cashews are low in sugar and very rich in fiber, unsaturated fats, and non-heme (plant) protein. Cashews are an excellent source of copper, magnesium, and manganese. The nutrients found in cashews are great for energy production, brain health, immunity, and bone health. These are a little higher in carbohydrates but can still fit into a low-carb diet when consumed in small amounts.

Macadamia Nuts: These nuts are an excellent choice for those on a low-carb diet. They are a great energy source with a high level of healthy monounsaturated fat. Macadamia nuts are lower in carbohydrates and higher in fat content. They are also packed with excellent phytonutrients, including monosaturated fat, fiber, manganese, thiamine, copper, magnesium, non-heme iron, and vitamin B6.

Hazelnuts: Hazelnuts are packed with phytonutrients but have a higher carb content, making them harder to fit into a low-carb diet. If you are on a Mediterranean or whole-food diet, these are quite workable and full of nutrients. Hazelnuts contain vitamin B6, folate, phosphorus, potassium, and zinc. They're a rich source of mono and polyunsaturated fats, omega-6 and omega-9 fatty acids, such as oleic acid. They have excellent health benefits, including decreasing blood fat levels, regulating blood pressure, reducing inflammation, and improving blood sugar levels.

Pecans: Pecans are not only delicious; they have some great health benefits too! Research suggests that pecans improve heart health and brain function and control blood sugar. A 1 oz serving of pecans (20 halves) contains saturated fat, fiber, over 19 vitamins and minerals, including non-heme (plant) protein, vitamin A, folate, niacin, riboflavin, thiamine, vitamin B6, vitamin E, calcium, potassium, and zinc.

Pine Nuts: These little nuts are not only delicious in pesto, but they are highly nutritious! What are the health benefits of pine nuts? These nuts lower lipid levels in the blood, reduce the risk of heart disease and act as an antioxidant. They aid with weight loss, lower blood pressure, and protect the liver and kidneys. They are stocked with vitamins and nutrients such as vitamin K, phosphorus, magnesium, zinc, and manganese (contributing to bone health). Pine nuts are also high in polyunsaturated fat, vitamins B1 and E, and minerals such as iron and copper. Pine nuts are also a great source of fiber, potassium, and vitamins B2 and B3. However, although these are packed with great nutrition, you will want to consume them sparingly as they are high in carbohydrates.

Pistachios: Pistachios are known to promote healthy gut bacteria. They are high in fiber, which acts as a prebiotic (increasing gut health), lowers blood pressure and cholesterol levels, improves blood sugar levels, improves blood vessel health, promotes eye health, and aids weight loss.

Pistachios are packed with minerals such as potassium, phosphorus, magnesium, calcium, and vitamins such as vitamins A, E, C, B (except B12), K, and folate.

Walnuts: Walnuts are rich in antioxidants and are a great source of omega 3, decreasing inflammation in the body. They also promote healthy gut flora, are cancer-protective, support weight loss, and help manage your risk for type 2 diabetes and cardiovascular disease.

The Case Against Peanuts: I did not add peanuts to this list because they are legumes, not nuts. I don't usually recommend peanuts because of some adverse health issues. Here are some of the things that concern me about peanuts:

1. Peanuts contain high levels of lectins. Lectins are nature's pesticide. They can damage our gut barrier cells and cause intestinal permeability (leaky gut). A leaky gut causes inflammation in the body, leading to autoimmune and chronic diseases like rheumatoid, lupus, IBS, Crohn's, colitis, and thyroiditis.
2. Peanuts contain a lot of phytic acid. Phytic acid binds to minerals and prevents the absorption of iron, calcium, magnesium, and zinc in the body, making peanuts anti-nutritious.

3. Peanuts/peanut butter are high in aflatoxins. Aflatoxins are naturally occurring toxic byproducts of fungal metabolism. A regular high dose of peanuts and peanut products may build this toxin up in your body, affecting your liver, causing cirrhosis and hepatitis B, and may lead to the development of cancer of the liver.

4. Peanuts can be highly allergic to some. The allergy to peanuts is the fastest-growing food allergy in North America. Allergic reactions to peanuts may cause anaphylaxis.

5. Peanut oil should not be used due to industrial solvents used to extract the oils from the peanuts. Peanut oil is extracted by dousing peanuts with hexane (a petroleum-based solvent), which can cause nervous system damage, pneumonitis (respiratory inflammation), and dizziness.

6. Peanuts are high in oxalates. In fact, they are brimming with these naturally occurring compounds. Oxalates trigger kidney stone formation, increasing inflammation and inflammatory bowel disease. Overconsumption of peanuts can trigger both fibromyalgia and contributes to anemia (due to the phytic acid).

7. Peanut farmers use toxic herbicides and pesticides to protect their crops. Peanut shells are soft and very absorbent, which makes them defenseless to diseases and fungi. Farmers use herbicides and fungicides like glyphosate (which causes kidney disease) and BP (which causes thyroid problems);

these products can leak into the peanut and lead to various cancers and DNA damage.

8. Peanuts are protease inhibitors. Protease inhibitors prevent our gut enzymes from breaking down proteins into amino acids. This causes elevated levels of the enzyme "trypsin." Trypsin triggers the loosening of the cell junctions, causing increased inflammation in the body.

9. What is peanuts' nutritional downside, and why should you switch to other nut and seed butters? Peanut butter is high in sugar, sodium, and trans fat and contains unnecessary food additives. Here are some of the other ingredients: high fructose corn syrup, dextrose, and maltodextrin. Peanut butter also contains hydrogenated vegetable oils, which directly affect the heart. I tell clients to drop the peanut butter and go for organic nut and seed butter. Organic nut and seed butters are much healthier products. My favorite is "Nature's Nut and Seed Butter," but many other great products exist.

How to choose the freshest and best source of nuts:

1. When you can, buy nuts still in their shells. They are fresher and will last longer.

2. Choose nuts that look fresh.

3. Avoid choosing nuts that appear shriveled, moldy, bruised, or smell rancid (rotten).

4. Choose plain nuts and organic when possible. Skip the sugar-coated and salted nuts. You don't need the added sugar or salt; these are poor quality.

5. Skip the bulk nuts in bins. They may be cheaper, but nuts stored in bins are not always fresh. Some stores don't properly rotate; they just add fresh nuts to the old nuts. Nuts only stay fresh in "sealed" bins and are only good for up to a month in a grocery store bin. You don't want to be consuming rancid nuts. The other factor with bulk binned nuts is that there may be bacteria from human contact or pests if they are not tightly sealed.
6. If you can't get the nuts fresh, buying packaged and sealed nuts with a packaged expiry date is best. Then, once opened, store them properly.

How to store nuts to contain freshness and nutrient values:

1. Store nuts in an airtight container in a cool, dry place; the refrigerator is the best option.
2. If you must store them at room temperature, store them away from direct light or warm places (this breeds mold and bacteria). Try to use them up within three months; I don't suggest keeping them longer.
3. Nuts freeze well. If you are keeping nuts for baking, crush them, place them in an air-tight container, and keep them in the freezer.

Some people are concerned that nuts may make you fat due to their high-fat content. Nuts won't make you fat! We have already covered why our body needs fat. Let's look at some research.

Research Title: Are Fatty Nuts A Weighty Concern?

A systematic review, meta-analysis, and dose-response meta-regression of prospective cohorts and randomized controlled trials.

Results of the Study: "Meta-regression showed that higher nut intake was associated with reductions in body weight and body fat. Current evidence demonstrates the concern that nut consumption contributes to increased adiposity appears unwarranted."

Summary below:

- According to research from the USDA, when eaten in their whole form, nuts like almonds could contribute up to 32% fewer calories than listed on their nutrition label due to their bioavailability and how the body absorbs their nutrients.
- **Brazil Nuts:** "Brazil nuts are an excellent source of selenium—just one Brazil nut provides 100% of your daily needs!"
- **Walnuts:** "Just eating 1 to 2 ounces of walnuts daily can help reduce the risk of developing Type 2 diabetes and heart disease."
- **Macadamia Nuts:** They are associated with lower cholesterol because of their rich monounsaturated fat content. Since high cholesterol can be a concern on a

long-term keto diet, macadamia nuts are an excellent choice to add.

- **Pecans:** Pecans have a 5:1 ratio of fat to carbs. Pecans pack sizable amounts of fiber and healthy unsaturated fats. "Fiber helps stabilize blood sugar levels and promotes weight loss by contributing to satiety," says Brownstein. "One small randomized controlled trial of people aged 40 to 80 with stable coronary artery disease found that eating 30 grams (the equivalent of 1 ounce) of pecans daily for 12 weeks reduced the ratio of total cholesterol to HDL (good).

- **Hazelnuts:** When choosing the best nuts for keto, thinking about their net carbs (AKA total carbs minus fiber) can be helpful. "Hazelnuts contain less than 2 grams of net carbs per ounce serving, making them a great choice for a keto diet. They are also one of the richest nut sources of monounsaturated fatty acids, which helps keep your heart healthy."

- **Pine Nuts:** Pine nuts are some of the highest-fat choices at around 19.4 grams per 1-ounce serving. This fat has a lot going for it beyond promoting ketosis. "Pine nuts are rich in pinolenic acid (PNLA), a fatty acid with many health benefits," says Bischof. "Pinolenic acid may lower cholesterol levels and even reduce inflammation."

Seeds

What about seeds? Are they important? Seeds are a great source of non-heme (plant) protein and healthy fats (polyunsaturated) and are loaded with fiber. Seeds also contain vitamins and minerals, including B1, B2, B3, vitamin E, magnesium, potassium, calcium, plant iron and zinc. The oilier the seed, the more antioxidants they contain. Seeds and a healthy whole-food diet can protect your body against heart disease, diabetes, and cancer. Seeds are an essential part of the human diet.

Let's look at the different types of seeds and what they offer:

Pumpkin Seeds: Pumpkin seeds are rich in magnesium and contain healthy fats and fiber. They may increase male fertility and lower the risk of breast cancer. They also support bladder and prostate health, promote heart health, are an oxidant (cancer-protective), and can improve sleep. Pumpkin seeds are full of vitamins such as vitamins B1, B2, B3, B5, B6, B9, C, E, and K. These seeds also contain minerals like calcium, iron, magnesium, manganese, phosphorus, potassium, sodium, and zinc. The carb content of pumpkin seeds is very low, so they fit in well on a keto diet.

Flax Seeds: Flax seeds are known to improve gut health and digestion and may relieve constipation. Flax seeds also lower total cholesterol levels LDL, making them heart-protective. Flax seeds also work as an anti-inflammatory agent. For women, this seed has some added benefits: it helps to manage menopausal symptoms, lessens menstrual cramps, and aids in maintaining healthy skin and hair. Flax seeds carry great fats (ALA and Omega 3's) and contain vitamins and nutrients. They are also a great source of thiamine, copper, magnesium, phosphorus, and molybdenum. Flax seeds should be bought fresh and in whole form. They should be ground just before eating. This maximizes the nutrient value and prevents the oils from going rancid. Buy fresh and grind fresh. Eating whole flax seeds is not the best practice as our bodies cannot properly digest them, so we grind them and add them to our food.

Sesame Seeds: Sesame seeds contribute a lot to our health! Adding a few sesame seeds to your daily diet can help your body in the following ways: it lowers cholesterol levels, fights infections, aids in oral health, is an antioxidant, improves heart health, increases natural immunity, and helps control diabetes. There are many vitamins and minerals found in this little snack.

- Vitamins: B1, B3, B2, B6, and B9.
- Minerals: phosphorous, magnesium, iron, zinc, molybdenum, and selenium.

So, bake with some sesame seeds and sprinkle them on your foods (especially salads).

Poppy Seeds: Poppy seeds are high in fiber. They are also effective at reducing the levels of LDL cholesterol. These seeds are rich in plant iron and improve blood circulation. They also help with eye health, lowering blood pressure, assisting in pain relief, helping with sleep, reducing kidney stones, and improving mental health. Poppy seeds have some great nutrient value. Here are a few:

- Fiber
- Manganese
- Copper
- Calcium
- Magnesium
- Phosphorus
- Zinc
- Thiamine

Note: Poppy seeds won't intoxicate you; however, poppy seed food products may lead to positive urine drug test results for opiates due to the hypersensitivity of these tests.

***Risk of Poppy Seeds:** Poppy seeds can contain trace opioid compounds. Medical experts recommend limiting the number of raw poppy seeds one eats to about 1 tbsp per 7 pounds of body weight. This means that someone who weighs 150 lbs. should not consume more than 7 tbsp of raw poppy seeds at a time. So, enjoy them in a limited quantity.

Sunflower Seeds: Sunflower seeds have numerous health benefits! Here are some:

- Boost immunity
- Lower cholesterol
- Protect the heart
- Lower the risk of cancer
- Manage diabetes
- Increase brain function
- Aid with weight loss
- Increase energy
- Good for skin
- Lower inflammation

Sunflower seeds are loaded with great vitamin and mineral sources like vitamin E, vitamin B1, vitamin B6, non-heme iron, copper, selenium, manganese, zinc, and potassium.

Sunflower seeds are a really great snack in salads or on their own. Next time you're out on a hike or road trip, bring a pack of organic sunflower seeds along for the ride!

Chia Seeds: Chia seeds are an excellent source of fiber. Increased fiber improves heart health, reduces cholesterol levels, and promotes gut and intestinal health. Fiber takes longer to digest and increases satiation. Chia seeds can play a role in weight loss and decreasing your risk of diabetes and heart disease.

Chia seeds are another seed carrying a punch of nutritional value. The hard-hitting nutrients are manganese, phosphorus, copper, selenium, magnesium, and calcium. Plant iron and zinc are also found in chia seeds, but they have reduced levels due to the phytic acid found in chia seeds.

***Caution with Chia seeds:** Due to the high fiber content, chia seeds in excess may cause constipation, diarrhea, bloating, or gas. They may also aggravate inflammatory bowel conditions like IBS and Crohn's disease, so avoid them if you have these ailments.

***Choking Hazard:** Dry chia seeds absorb water. If ingested dry, they will swell up and become gelatinous; this could cause choking or obstruction. Always soak these seeds for 20 minutes before consuming.

How to Consume Chia Seeds: We mainly consume chia by turning them into a keto chia pudding. Another way to consume them is to add whole or ground chia seeds to milk, yogurt, or baked items.

How to Choose Seeds:

1. Buy your seeds as fresh as possible and keep them in their whole form (unless flax). The pre-grinding

of seeds will devalue many nutrients and oils, so grind your whole seeds as needed.

Notes: Flax seeds are difficult for the body to break down when they are whole, so this seed is always the best fresh ground for your food.

2. Always check the dates on your seeds to ensure freshness, and when possible, buy organic.
3. Avoid any pre-salted or sugared seeds.

Storing Seeds

1. Poorly stored seeds may have become oxidized, contain bugs, be moldy, smell rancid, or have a slimy feel. If that occurs, your seeds have gone bad and must be thrown out.
2. To keep your seeds fresh and maintain their nutrient value, keep them "whole," not "ground" in an airtight container. Storing them in the fridge is the best practice, but most seeds can also be kept in a cool cupboard that is out of sunlight and away from heat in a sealed container.
3. Skip the bulk seeds in bins. They may be cheaper, but seeds stored in bins are not always fresh. Some stores don't rotate properly. Seeds only stay fresh in "sealed" bins and are nutritionally best for around 60 days (if stored properly). You don't want to be consuming rancid seeds. The issue with bulk binned seeds is that there may be bacteria in there from human contact or rodents/bugs.

Conclusion: This chapter shows that nuts and seeds are a wonderful way to increase nutrition. However, you must have the "nutritional foundation" of good eating habits for this to work properly. Focus on a fresh, whole-food diet with lots of clean water, proper sleep, and exercise; these little snacks will top you up nutritionally.

Summary of Chapter 7

Nuts and seeds should be an important part of our diet. Of course, if you have nut or seed sensitivity or allergies, avoid them. However, the benefits of snacking on nuts and seeds to top up our nutritional needs are very concrete. Nuts are also rich in vitamins and minerals, such as vitamin E, B6, niacin and folate, magnesium, zinc, plant iron, calcium, copper, selenium, phosphorus, and potassium.

Seeds are a great source of (plant) protein, healthy fats, and fiber. Seeds also contain B1, B2, B3, vitamin E, magnesium, potassium, calcium, plant iron, and zinc. Both nuts and seeds have antioxidant properties.

1. Nuts and seeds have a great balance of our macros.
2. The fat in nuts and seeds is "good fats" and helps reduce weight, lower the risk of cardiovascular disease and type 2 diabetes, lower inflammation, and keep you satiated.

3. If you are on a low-carb or keto diet, eat nuts with a lower carb count, like almonds, macadamis, pecans, and brazil nuts. All seeds are fine.
4. Pay attention to some of the chia and poppy seeds cautions.
5. Make sure you are buying the freshest nuts and seeds. Don't consume nuts or seeds past the due dates, and avoid bulk-stored nuts and seeds.
6. Proper storage for nuts and seeds is important. When possible, store them in an airtight container in the refrigerator. Next best storage place is an airtight container in a cool cupboard away from heat and light. Remember to eat fresh nuts before three months and seeds before two months.

Takeaway from Chapter 7:

Nuts and seeds are an excellent additive to a fresh, whole foods diet. Ensure they are fresh, organic when possible, stored properly, and only ground before eating.

Now, go grab a handful of nuts and seeds and enjoy!

Nuts and Seeds

Chapter 8 Sugar: The Poison We Don't Talk About

No food concerns me more than sugar. As a nutritionist, I see more damage done to the human body by our society's overconsumption of sugar than anything else. Sugar in large amounts can be as toxic as alcohol and as addictive as cocaine. If we were to do what other countries are toying with, trying to ban both sugar and high fructose corn syrup, we would alleviate the backlog in our medical and dental systems. We would see mental, physical, and dental health drastically improve. It's been years since I have consumed sugar (except for fruit/vegetables). I am cautious to avoid any product with added sugar or high fructose corn syrup. Seeing the incredible improvements in my mental clarity, energy levels, body weight, teeth, and skin, I refused to return to a high-sugar diet.

It may seem like a radical decision for significant sugar consumers. However, when you speak to those who have chosen to eliminate sugar entirely from their diet (and there are many of us), they will tell you similar health stories. I have had people say to me that living without sugar is "not possible" and that it's "unsustainable." They will say, "You must live in the real world." After over two decades of being sugar-free (added sugar), I can assure you that it is quite possible and gratifying. We still bake, eat ice cream, and have treats, but they are homemade without sugar. We use crushed fruit and cream, stevia leaves, and sometimes monk fruit. The chocolate we eat is bitter, 85-95% natural cacao. We still *really* enjoy our food, and what we make is delicious! The trick is surviving the first two weeks of cravings and giving your taste buds time to readapt to natural whole foods. The rest is learning how to do recipes differently and read labels. It becomes easy and repetitive once you have your shopping and meals set.

Let me share the information and research that brought me to this radical decision. At the end of this chapter, I will give you some concrete steps to kick the sugar habit, so buckle up, and let's look at "sugar."

How Much Sugar Did Our Great-Grandparents Eat?

In the 1800s, sugar in the human diet was still relatively low because people mostly lived off what they grew. Sugar was purchased sparingly as a treat, and the sugar industry had not yet come to fruition. However, by the early 1900s, sugar had become more of a household staple. Sugar production was becoming a profitable, growing industry.

In 1800, the average North American consumed 22.4 grams (5.5 tsp) of sugar daily through natural food (not added sugar). When I say natural foods, I mean vegetables, fruits, grains, and honey. By the late 1900s, sugar consumption had risen to around 112 grams daily (28 tsp). This was when we started seeing all the various types of sugar becoming popular. By the 2000s, sugar consumption rose to about 227 grams (56 tsp) daily. That seems impossible, but if you begin reading labels, you will find that sugar is added to almost every food and beverage product. Today, the "sugar bus" is headed off a cliff. We see our society dealing with a wide variety of medical and dental situations due to our overconsumption of one thing: "sugar."

The Excess Consumption of Sugar Has Had Some Very Adverse Health Effects on Society

Along with the incredible increase in sugar and sugar addiction (it's a real thing) comes a host of new "food-related diseases" (food-related means that the food we eat is causing us ill health). Our great-grandparents did not see food-related diseases such as NAFLD (non-alcoholic fatty liver disease), metabolic syndrome, or insulin resistance syndrome. We must also look at the rate at which we see some diseases we know will increase.

- Type 2 diabetes in the 1800s to mid-1950s was only seen in older adults who were in poor health. Today, we are seeing children as young as ten who are developing type 2 diabetes. One in ten children is obese and quickly becoming pre-diabetic or diabetic. All of this is caused by food, such as simple carbs, ultra-processed foods, sugar, and sugary drinks.

- Heart disease between 1800 and 1950 was relatively low, primarily found in elderly men or those wealthy few who were morbidly obese. Today, cardiovascular disease is the number one killer among men, women, and even some youths. We are seeing heart attacks in young people being linked to the rise of sedentary lifestyles, poor food choices, excessive sugar, energy drinks, radical sleep patterns, and societal stress.
- Cancer rates between 1800 and 1900 were lower. Even though cancer was present years ago, it was rarer than today. Today, cancer is the second leading killer disease in North America. There is a direct link between obesity (being overweight) and various cancers. This is caused mainly by a sedentary lifestyle, consuming a high sugar (simple carb) diet, having chronic sleep issues, high-stress levels, and being exposed to various environmental chemicals and food additives.

It's easy to see that our convenient "fast food" culture is killing us at an alarming rate. However, there is good news. We can educate ourselves. We can regain our power and change our health and lifestyle to make us flourish. The power of health is in our own hands. Your body is fantastic at healing, but it has to begin with your food and lifestyle decisions. You are the one responsible for your own body. You cannot take a pill, supplement, or herb to "get healthy" without first appropriately changing your diet. A proper diet lays the foundation; you can add supplements and herbs to that great foundation. If you are eating pure junk, taking supplements is not going to change your health drastically. They may cancel each other out.

When I speak about nutrition, I like to break things down to the sugar amounts we find in foods we regularly consume. Most people find the results shocking when they see how much sugar is in their food. Below is a sample of a former client's healthy "low-fat" breakfast. He was in his mid-50s and pre-diabetic, had poor cholesterol markers, and was following a very low-fat diet. Let's look at the sugar content of just that one meal.

Breakfast:

- Low-fat fruit yogurt (23 g of sugar)
- Banana (12 grams of sugar)
- Two whole wheat toasts (3.2 g of sugar)
- Strawberry jam (2 pkg 14 g sugar)
- 8 oz glass of orange juice (23 g of sugar)
- Flavored coffee from Starbucks white chocolate mocha (53 g of sugar)

Total: 128.2 grams of sugar (32.05 teaspoons of sugar)

This person hadn't even had lunch, dinner, or snacks yet. The sugars add up very quickly. He was following a "low fat" "heart healthy" diet given to him by his hospital dietitian. His fat content for breakfast was low; however, when a product is low fat, it's always high in sugar! This client's daily sugar intake was around 325 grams (81.25 tsp.) of sugar a day. However, he was staying within his recommended fat grams of 30 per day. When he came to me, he was having difficulty losing weight and was constantly hungry.

Note: The liver can only process around 6 tsp of "natural" sugar daily (24 grams). I would suggest less. That amount (24 grams) works if you are a healthy, active, or growing child. However, for those who are overweight, obese, or have other health issues, I suggest closer to 3-4 tsp a day (12-16 g) until your body comes back to good health.

What do the professionals recommend as an acceptable level of sugar?

Diabetes Canada Recommendation? The recommended daily limit set by Diabetes Canada is no more than 50 grams (12 tsp.) of **free** sugar a day. Holistic Nutritionists find this very high for the general population of healthy individuals and especially for diabetic clients.

The American Heart Association recommends that American males stay under nine teaspoons of sugar (36 g) daily and six teaspoons of sugar daily for women (24 g).

The World Health Organization recommends sugar intake be kept at approximately six teaspoons per day (24 g). Amazingly, that is almost half the sugar that Diabetes Canada recommends for diabetics. Strange, isn't it?

Let's compare that to the countries with the lowest amount of sugar in their diet. Uganda consumes approximately 2 grams of sugar per day. Myanmar consumes around 3 grams of sugar per day.

So, what is the cost of this excessive sugar consumption?

Let's look at the cost of diabetes in Canada as per Canada.ca (the government sight). This piece was written on the Canada.ca news release on May 30, 2023 (Ottawa, Ontario) by the Patented Medicine Prices Review Board.

"This fourth report in the Market Intelligence series analyzes the market for drugs used in the treatment of diabetes. It is estimated that 5.7 million Canadians have diagnosed and undiagnosed diabetes, and another 6 million Canadians are likely pre-diabetic. The cost burden of diabetes in Canada is around $29 billion annually."

Does anyone else find it interesting that the Diabetes Canada organization is setting the daily recommendation for sugar so high (50 g) yet pointing clients towards pharmaceuticals? The only ones winning here are the pharmaceutical companies. Would it not be easier and more health-conscious to suggest dietary/lifestyle changes and the removal of excess sugar from the diet? Just saying.

The Debate on Sugar: John Yudkin, Dr. Robert Lustig, and Other Research

The first chapter discussed the hypothesis debate between John Yudkin (England) and Ancel Keys (USA) in the 1900s. After President Eisenhower's heart attack, the search went on to find the contributing factor to heart disease. Ancel Keys' did a seven-country research study (originally based on 22 countries) and hypothesized that saturated fat was causing cardiovascular disease.

Around the same time, in England, John Yudkin was working on a hypothesis proving that sugar led to diabetes and heart disease, not fat. Keys' went after Yudkin's hypothesis and basically shut him down. The American Heart Association adopted the Keys' Lipid Hypothesis shortly after, and fat became vilified. For decades, North America has pushed the low-fat, high-carb diet, and we have seen diabetes, heart disease and cancer skyrocket. Later on, it was found that Keys' original research notes disproved his lipid hypothesis.

You can find a link to John Yudkin's hypothesis in his original book *"Pure, White and Deadly"* online. I would strongly urge you to read through it. The forwarding was done by Dr. Robert Lustig (MD, MSL Professor emeritus of Pediatrics, Division of Endocrinology at the University of California, San Francisco). Dr. Lustig is a world-renowned speaker who is the leading expert on the harms of sugar.

A second article worth reading is in the "The Guardian" titled "The Sugar Conspiracy." Dr. Lustig's research of what sugar does to the human body is laid out in his book *"Sugar: The Bitter Truth."* This article reflects some of the content in that book and the research that Dr Lustig has found.

CNN (Life/Food) Updated 7:11 PM EDT, Wed April 5, 2023

"In a large review of 73 meta-analyses (which included 8,601 studies), high consumption of added sugar was associated with significantly higher risks of 45 negative health outcomes, including diabetes, gout, obesity, high blood pressure, heart attack, stroke, cancer, asthma, tooth decay, depression, and early death."

We will always find professionals who can lean on either side of this "sugar vs. fat debate." However, I definitely err on the side of Dr. Lustig. I have seen the success of going sugar-free in my own health. I have also seen the health benefits that have appeared in clients as they have turned to a sugar-free, whole-food diet. I would strongly suggest that you take the time to do a deep dive into the research on the effects of sugar yourself and come to your conclusion. As for me, I would recommend that people stay away from added sugar, processed foods, candy and sweets, sugary drinks, and juicing fruits. There are better ways to eat and some delicious sweet alternatives out there. Eat real fresh food!

How Does Sugar Affect Your Organs? (Liver, Pancreas, Heart, Brain)

Sugar and the Liver:

The liver is one of the most vital organs in our body; it performs over 500 functions. The two essential functions are filtering our blood and breaking down poisonous and toxic substances, such as alcohol, sugar, pharmaceuticals, etc. The liver also produces bile, which helps digest fats and removes waste. If our liver does not work correctly, we literally have no "filtration" system. This can lead to various metabolic issues within our body. An excess of refined sugar and high-fructose corn syrup causes a fatty buildup that can lead to liver disease (NAFLD-Non-Alcoholic Fatty Liver Disease), which can then lead to advanced liver disease. A perfectly "healthy" liver can only handle approximately 6 tsp (24 g) of natural sugar (fructose included) per day. While the liver becomes overwhelmed with excess sugar, it becomes sluggish. It stops filtering our blood properly, and toxins will begin to accumulate. That excess sugar will also lead to visceral fat (fat accumulating around the internal organs), which will cause some very adverse health outcomes. I would suggest closer to 3 tsp (12 g) a day for those who are obese, have metabolic syndrome, are insulin resistant, have diabetes, problems associated with inflammation, or other more severe health concerns.

Sugar and the Pancreas:

The pancreas is another vital organ. The pancreas' role is to deal with various hormones, especially glucagon and insulin. Our pancreas maintains blood glucose levels within the small range of 4-6 mm. The pancreas preserves this range by the opposing and balanced actions of glucagon and insulin. We call this glucose homeostasis. So, when we flood the pancreas with extra sugar, high-sugary foods, and excess fructose, it will know our glucose levels are off balance. The outcome of this imbalance can cause insulin sensitivity, insulin resistance, type 2 diabetes, metabolic issues, and even pancreatic cancer.

Sugar and the Heart:

Most people do not realize that excess sugar/fructose also contributes to heart disease; it definitely does. Did you know excess sugar/fructose can raise LDL and triglycerides and lower your HDL? Over time, this can lead to a greater visceral (organ) fat accumulation, which may turn into fatty liver disease. Fatty liver disease will raise your risk of heart disease. A high-sugar diet also increases blood pressure and creates excess inflammation in the body. Both high blood pressure and inflammation lead to heart disease and stroke.

Sugar and the Brain: Type 3 Diabetes

Chronic high blood sugar (hyperglycemia) causes damage to the blood vessels in the brain that carry oxygen-rich blood. Brain cells die when your brain loses blood flow (brain atrophy). Brain atrophy (brain shrinkage) will cause problems with cloudy thinking and memory issues, which may lead to vascular dementia or stroke.

Alzheimer's/Dementia: Type 3 diabetes is being used by some professionals as a new term for Alzheimer's. Research is currently being done on the link between hyperglycemia (diabetes) and Alzheimer's (a form of dementia). We know that chronic sugar/fructose intake affects memory and the brain's health, so it is viable research. A type of insulin resistance triggers dementia. The cause is insulin-like growth factor dysfunction, specifically in the brain. Some clients in the early stages of Alzheimer's have seen the benefits of following a ketogenic diet and the addition of MCT oil or Coconut oil as part of their treatment plan. The ketogenic eating plan is low carb, with a trace amount of natural sugar and good essential fats that feed the brain. Currently, more research is being done on the ketogenic diet and dementia.

What Diseases are Triggered by Overconsumption of Sugar?

There are specific food-related diseases currently caused by poor eating, such as excess sugar/fructose and a highly processed diet. Most of these diseases were not seen in our great-grandparents' era. Let's look at how the rates of these food-related diseases have risen over the past 30 years.

Obesity rates in North America: Stats are provided by Harvard T.H. Chan (School of Public Health),

"Obesity rates in the USA have more than doubled since 1980. They remain the highest of all of the first-world countries. Two out of three American adults are overweight or obese (69 %), and one out of three are obese. This is a direct relation to poor nutritional choices, high sugar consumption, and inactivity.

Canada does not fare a lot better. In 1979, 14 % of Canadian adults were obese. By 2008, 25 % of adults were obese, and 62 % were overweight or obese. The obesity rate actually went up during the high-carb, low-fat era of eating."

*Remember, fat was vilified from the 1960s to the 2000s thanks to the Ancel Keys' hypothesis. Sugar was deemed "good," even necessary for our bodies to function. We are now seeing the proof in that failed theory.

Unfortunately, that theory has corrupted our food system and is killing our people.

Diabetes

Let's look at the worldwide rate of diabetes from 1980 to 2014. According to NCBI (National Center for Biotechnology Information) (PMC5081106), *"The number of adults with diabetes in the world increased from 108 million in 1980 to 422 million in 2014 (figure 7). East Asia and South Asia had the largest rises of absolute numbers and had the largest number of people with diabetes in 2014: 106 million and 86 million, respectively."*

When we remove fat from the human diet and replace it with simple carbohydrates (sugar), we set up our population for the perfect storm of illness. Our bodies require fat (for brain health and hormones) and heme protein (animals that bleed) to build blood and muscle. When Canada and the USA lowered the amount of meat (heme protein), we did ourselves a disservice as protein keeps us satiated, improves our ability to make blood, and helps to maintain our blood sugar levels (as does fat). They told us to remove the fat that our brains and hormones require and replace that with an almost all-carb diet. Of course, we would see a drastic spike in insulin issues like diabetes.

Heart Disease

A diet high in sugar and simple carbohydrates has been linked to the rising of inflammation, LDL cholesterol, and higher levels of Triglycerides. These are known to clog arteries that supply oxygen to the heart. This, in turn, causes high blood pressure. High-sugar diets are directly linked to high blood pressure, which increases the risk of both heart disease and stroke. Sugar causes weight gain, visceral (organ fat), inflammation, and dental issues and will eventually affect your heart.

NAFLD (Non-Alcoholic Fatty Liver Disease)

The liver is the largest organ in our body. Some critical functions of the liver are removing toxins from our blood system, balancing blood sugar levels, emulsifying fat, and regulating blood clotting factors. So, it is the gatekeeper of our system. Fructose (sugar) can be problematic for the liver to process. It should be kept at a maximum ingestion of 6 tsp (24 g) of "natural" sugar (natural sugar is sugar that comes from vegetables, fruit, dairy, and grains). Therefore, any extra sugar from simple carbs, candy, junk food, sugary drinks, and baked goods will tax the liver.

How does a diet high in sugar and simple carbs affect the liver? We all know how sugar affects the body (obesity and dental issues), but did you know that carbohydrates are directly turned into sugar within the liver and then stored as fat if not burned up via exercise? Fructose is stored as visceral fat (fat around the vital organs). Excessive amounts of sugar and fructose cause a fatty buildup around the liver, making it function poorly. This can directly lead to non-alcoholic fatty liver disease (NAFLD) and can further lead to serious liver diseases like NASH (Non-alcoholic steatohepatitis) and Cirrhosis of the liver.

Metabolic Syndrome

Metabolic syndrome is a food-related disease caused by diets high in carbohydrates, simple carbs, excess sugar, ultra-processed foods, and lack of exercise. Metabolic syndrome is a cluster of conditions that all occur simultaneously. These conditions include high blood pressure, high blood sugar (A1C), excess body fat around the waist, abnormal cholesterol (high LDL), and elevated triglyceride levels. Metabolic syndrome increases your risk of heart disease, stroke, and type 2 diabetes.

Insulin Resistance:

Insulin resistance is another "food-related" disease. Insulin resistance occurs when the cells in your muscles, fat, and liver stop responding to insulin and can't easily take up glucose from your blood. This causes your pancreas to make more insulin to help glucose enter your cells. What are the symptoms of Insulin Resistance?

- Extreme thirst or hunger
- Feeling hungry right after meals
- Frequent urination
- Tingling in hands/feet
- Fatigue
- Low immunity
- Frequent infections
- High A1C and fasting glucose numbers
- Similar to type 2 diabetes symptoms seen in pre-diabetic clients.

Both insulin resistance and metabolic syndrome can be reversed relatively quickly by using a ketogenic diet, which removes simple carbohydrates, sugar, and ultra-processed foods while increasing good fats, good quality heme proteins, nuts and seeds, vegetables, and low-carb fruit (greens, brightly colored vegetables, and berries).

Alzheimer's (Type 3 Diabetes):

New research is currently being done on the effects of diabetes mellitus and the brain as it pertains to dementia/Alzheimer's. More research needs to be done, but the evidence appears to strongly suggest that there is a link between the consumption of excess sugar and diabetes mellitus and dementia/Alzheimer's.

What are all the different forms of sugar? Let's summarize the various types of sugar into seven general forms and where they are found.

- Fructose is found in honey and fruits.
- Galactose is found in milk and dairy.
- Glucose is found in fruits, honey, high fructose corn syrup, and vegetables.
- Lactose is found in milk (glucose and galactose).
- Maltose is found in barley.
- Sucrose is found in plants (glucose and fructose).
- Xylose is found in wood/straw.

Hidden Sugars: Sugar is Often Hidden in Foods Under Various Names

Would you be surprised to find that there are roughly 65 different names of sugar? Look at these hidden sugars next time you read a label. Some companies want to make their product "appear" healthy by disguising sugar under different names. For example, when a product label says it has 0 sugar but 50 grams of carbohydrates, you know there are hidden sugars!

- Anhydrous dextrose
- Agave
- Agave nectar
- Beet sugar

- Brown sugar (light and dark brown)
- Cane juice
- Cane juice solids
- Cane sugar
- Cane syrup
- Carob syrup
- Caster sugar
- Coconut sugar
- Confectioners' sugar
- Corn syrup
- Corn syrup solids
- Crystalline fructose
- Date sugar
- Demerara sugar
- Dextran
- Dextrose
- Dehydrated cane juice
- Evaporated cane juice
- Evaporated cane syrup
- Evaporated sugar cane
- Fructose
- Fructose crystals
- Fruit juice crystals
- Fruit juice concentrate
- Glazing sugar
- Glucose
- Glucose syrup
- Golden sugar
- Golden syrup
- Granulated sugar
- High-fructose corn syrup (HFCS)
- Honey

- Icing sugar
- Invert sugar
- Invert syrup
- King's syrup
- Lactose
- Maple syrup
- Maple sugar
- Maltose
- Malt sugar
- Malt syrup
- Molasses
- Muscovado
- Nectar
- Pancake syrup
- Panocha
- Powdered sugar
- Raw sugar
- Refiners' syrup
- Sorghum
- Sorghum syrup
- Sucanat
- Sucrose
- Sugar
- Superfine sugar
- Table sugar
- Treacle
- Turbinado sugar
- White sugar
- Yellow sugar

The Problem with High Fructose Corn Syrup, as per Dr. Lustig

Who is Dr. Robert Lustig? What is his view on High Fructose Corn Syrup?

Dr. Lustig is a neuroendocrinologist with expertise in metabolism, obesity, and nutrition. He's the Emeritus Professor of Pediatrics in the Division of Endocrinology and a member of the Institute for Health Policy Studies at UCSF. Dr. Lustig is one of the current leaders of the "anti-sugar" movement that is changing the food industry. He is the author of many books on this topic, such as *"Fat Chance"* and the foreword writer of John Yudkin's book *"Pure, White, and Deadly."* His latest book is *"Metabolical: The Lure and the Lies of Processed Food, Nutrition, and Modern Medicine."*

Dr. Lustig has been one of the leaders in the "sugar is toxic" movement. His professional view of sugar/fructose is that sugar is a toxic substance that people abuse. In Lustig's view, sugar should be in the same category as cigarettes and alcohol. He believes that excess sugar and fructose lays the foundation for many food-related diseases. The current research shows that when large quantities of fructose reach the liver, the liver uses excess fructose to create fat, a process called "lipogenesis." Therefore, people who consume too much fructose can develop non-alcoholic fatty liver disease, a condition in which too much fat is stored in the liver cells.

High fructose corn syrup (found in many food products) wreaks havoc on the human body. Studies show that high fructose corn syrup increases your appetite and leads to obesity quicker than regular sugar. "High fructose corn syrup" is a massive contributor to diabetes, inflammation, high LDL and triglycerides, insulin resistance, metabolic syndrome (NAFLD), non-alcoholic fatty liver disease, hypertension, and heart disease. Many countries have drastically reduced HFCS in their products due to its danger to the human body, including India, Ireland, Sweden, Austria, Uruguay, and Lithuania. The USA, China, and Canada are substantial corn producers and have not yet "decided" to look at lowering the consumption of HFCS in our products. They do not want the corn producers to lose money. However, we see the results in North America through the obesity epidemic, skyrocketing diabetes rates, and inflammation-related diseases.

Isn't honey, cane sugar, brown sugar, or corn syrup a healthier form of sugar?

I am asked the above question frequently. Many say, "I don't use table sugar; I use a healthier sweetener like honey, coconut sugar, corn syrup, cane sugar," and the list goes on. You may feel these are healthier forms of sugar, and companies tell you that, but they are not healthy when consumed in high amounts or daily. The liver sees all these sugars as "sugar." If you overconsume any of these sugar products, your liver will not know the difference and will become overwhelmed and clogged. Imagine someone saying, "I had three glasses of vodka last night because it's healthier than having three cocktails." Both are alcoholic products, and your liver will have to struggle to process either drink. Always keep in mind that your liver can only handle 6 tsp (24 g) of "natural sugar" a day.

What about sugar alcohols?

Sugar alcohols are sweeteners and have about half the calories of regular sugar. They are found naturally in certain fruits and vegetables; some may also be artificial and are added to processed foods to sweeten them.

In foods labeled "sugar-free" or "no sugar added," many add sugar alcohols. Look for these names on your labels: Erythritol, Maltitol, Mannitol, Sorbitol, Xylitol, Hydrogenated Starch Hydrolysates (HSH), and Isomalt. Often, food companies combine sugar alcohols and artificial sweeteners to make foods taste sweeter. Sugar alcohols in excess may have harmful side effects such as bloating, diarrhea, and disruption of your gut biome.

How Sugar Addiction Works with the Hormones Ghrelin and Leptin

It is challenging to give up sugar! Sugar is addictive for almost everyone, and your body can quickly become dependent on it. In fact, sugar has been proven to be more addictive than cocaine. Many struggle to give up sugar, and they blame themselves when they fail. Sugar is so addictive that when you have some, your brain will begin to crave more almost immediately. The more sugar you have in your diet, the hungrier you feel and the more cravings you have. This is actually due to a hormone called "Ghrelin."

We have three hormones that deal with food. We all know the hormone insulin, but most have never heard of "Ghrelin" or its sister "Leptin." Both Ghrelin and Leptin affect insulin sensitivity and glucose homeostasis. Ghrelin is the hormone that makes you hungry, crave food, and store fat. This hormone feeds off sugar, simple carbs, rice/grains, ultra-processed foods, and excessive fructose from fruit. When you consume high amounts of foods that spike Ghrelin, you are on a constant feedback loop that makes you crave more. You end up overeating due to an insatiable desire for simple carbs and sugar. You aren't craving chicken breasts and salads. You will want bread or sweets.

Now compare that to its sister, the hormone Leptin. "Leptin' is the hormone that subdues your hunger. This is the hormone that makes you feel full; it also aids in maintaining a healthy weight. Leptin feeds off good fats, heme protein (meat, fish, poultry, etc.), non-starch vegetables, lower-carb fruits, nuts, seeds, dairy, and eggs. Think about it: How easy is it to eat a bag of cookies or chips compared to eating a 10-oz steak? The calories may be similar; however, they turn on different hormones. The cookies and chips will stimulate the release of Ghrelin, while the steak will release Leptin.

This should console those who have repeatedly tried to cut down on sugar but failed. You are not weak, and you don't lack willpower. Quitting sugar is far from simple willpower. There are hormones involved that can sabotage your attempts to kick the habit.

So, for those who have consumed so much sugar that you have become dependent, you will need to kick the habit, and we will discuss how to do so shortly.

Are you addicted?

Two of the most frequent questions I am asked as a nutritionist are,

1. "Is it possible to be addicted to sugar?"
2. "How can I tell?"

Signs of Sugar Addiction:

Yes, it is very possible to be addicted to sugar! Most people can't really tell if they are in a state of addiction until they completely withdraw from the substance. This is because, with any addictive substance, you get used to the way it makes you feel. The symptoms of addiction become your "norm." If you stop sugar and feel no difference at all within your mind and body, then you are probably not addicted.

However, if you stop sugar cold turkey and your body reacts in any of the following ways, you have the proof that you are dependent on sugar and that dependency needs to be broken.

Sugar Withdrawal Symptoms

The removal of sugar from your diet causes the blood sugar levels to plummet, stressing the body and frustrating the Ghrelin hormone. At first, this will increase your cravings to eat sugar. However, this will only happen for a short time. Eventually, Leptin will increase while you eat Leptin-inspiring foods, and the sugar cravings will ultimately stop. On average, this may take a week or two, depending on how addicted you are. The symptoms of withdrawal may be all or some of the following:

- Anxiety and depression
- Bloating and diarrhea
- Cravings for junk food, desserts, sugar, sugary drinks
- Chills or involuntary shaking
- Headaches
- Fatigue
- Insomnia

Experiencing these symptoms after stopping sugar will expose your addiction to sugar. Fortunately, these symptoms are temporary and will pass.

How to break the sugar addiction?

I have developed a 6-step program to kick the sugar habit and begin to detox your body (especially your liver).

Step 1: Purge your home. Just as you would with alcohol, get rid of the sugar and products that have sugar or HFCS in them, and cleanse your home from any temptation because when the sugar cravings hit, you don't want to make it easy.

Step 2: Make a list of all your favorite (sugar-free) whole foods you can have. Focus on all those foods you can have instead of listing all the foods you cannot have. It puts more of a positive spin on your food journey. For example, what meat, fish, poultry, and heme protein do you love? What is your favorite full-fat (unflavored) dairy? What are your favorite nuts and seeds? Switch to a "lower carb bread" or an original grain bread and get a recipe to make cauliflower rice. What are your favorite berries that are low on the glycemic index? What are your favorite vegetables? If you do morning coffee with milk and sugar, switch to unflavored full-fat cream and stevia leaf or a shot of plain vanilla (not vanilla syrup).

Step 3: Go shopping and do some meal prep. If you prepare the appropriate food in your home beforehand, you will be less tempted to cheat or eat out. We make all our lunches and dinners for the week over the weekend. We keep the meals in our fridge in containers. This way, we can have our prepared meals during the day.

Step 4: Be mentally ready for some discomfort. If you are prepared mentally to know you will have some symptoms show up, you will be ready for them. Don't begin this journey at a busy time in your life. Make sure you don't have any big gatherings, holidays, or parties on your schedule for 2-3 weeks. Permit yourself to stay focused on detoxing.

Step 5: Drink plenty of water and herbal teas. Staying hydrated will make this process much more manageable. A great way to help clean out your liver a little would be to add some lemon wedges to your water.

Step 6: Sleep, de-stress, and journal. Your body will work hard to cleanse, so you will need to work on good sleep habits. Aim for 7-8 hours of sleep a night if possible. Also, find a way to de-stress. It may be a walk in nature, fishing, meditation, or prayer; just take some time for self-care. If you do like journaling, take time to journal how you are feeling each day. You will be amazed to see the results unfold. The first couple of days may be challenging, but as your mind clears, your skin clears, and your energy increases, you will have more exciting things to write about!

What are the best alternatives to using sugar?

Stevia: Stevia has zero calories and lowers blood pressure. It also doesn't affect the liver or pancreas. It is a leaf that you can grow naturally. Simply dry the leaves and crush them before using them. Ensure it is organic and not mixed with anything else when buying it. We use organic stevia leaf for baking, and I love it in coffee. You only need a tiny amount to sweeten things.

Erythritol: This sugar substitute can aid in weight loss and is safe for diabetics.

Xylitol: Two benefits of Xylitol are that it can aid digestion and promote dental health.

Monk Fruit: Monk fruit has anti-inflammatory properties and is safe for diabetics.

Important note: I would recommend the following

two sweeteners (honey and real maple syrup) for those who are not dealing with any medical conditions and are not obese. They are natural sugars and are whole foods and can be added to a healthy whole-food diet. However, honey and maple syrup are not the best for those who are pre-diabetic, diabetic, or insulin-resistant. Those who have metabolic syndrome or NAFLD should also choose one of the sugar alternatives instead.

Raw Honey: Raw honey can be an excellent addition to those who are healthy and on a whole foods or Mediterranean diet. Honey is known to lower cholesterol and is high in antioxidants.

Maple Syrup: Pure maple syrup can also be an excellent sweetener for those who are healthy. Maple syrup is high in antioxidants and contributes to good skin health.

Myth Buster: Most of us were taught that the body needs carbohydrates (and sugar).

Did you know that the body can function with little carbohydrates? The need for most of our diet to be carbohydrates is a misunderstanding of human anatomy. Although some "specific tissues" in the body have certain glucose requirements (the brain), these requirements are met by gluconeogenic sources within the body, even without dietary carbohydrates. When you lower the carbohydrates in your diet, the liver will create its supply of glucose. If you are eating Keto, carnivore, or low carb, your body will naturally produce the glucose it requires for the brain via the liver.

Summary of Chapter 8

In large quantities, sugar is toxic and leads to many food-related diseases.

1. Sugar is addictive and unnecessary, and when consumed in excess, it can damage your organs, brain, skin, and teeth.
2. Sugar affects all of our organs, not only the liver.
3. The liver is one of your most vital organs. It not only emulsifies fat; it also filters toxins from your body. The liver has difficulty breaking down alcohol, sugar (especially fructose), and poor-quality fats. The liver can only process roughly 6 tsp (24 g) of natural sugars (those found in whole foods). Any excess quantities of sugar can compromise the liver.
4. Sugar triggers diabetes, insulin resistance, metabolic syndrome, NAFLD, heart disease, tooth decay, and dementia.
5. There are seven types of sugar and over 65 names of sugar. Many products (even some that claim to be sugar-free) have sugar snuck in under other names, so read the list and read your labels.
6. Sugar is more addictive than cocaine, and today, it is found in almost every product, so stick with natural whole foods when possible.

7. Sugar addiction is not just a habit; it is a chemical dependency. Sugar dependency involves three hormones: Insulin, Ghrelin, and Leptin.
8. We can break the sugar addiction; it takes planning and dedication, and that change can renew your health. Follow the six-step plan.
9. There are some great alternatives to sugar: Stevia, Erythritol, Xylitol, and Monk fruit. Honey and pure maple syrup are good alternatives for healthy people following a whole foods or Mediterranean diet.
10. Your body does not require extra carbs (other than those from fruits and vegetables). The body makes its glucose (carbohydrates) via the liver. So even if you eat carnivore, Keto, or low carb, your body will produce the necessary glucose.

Takeaway from Chapter 8:

Yes, sugar and high fructose corn syrup are delicious. It makes many food products taste amazing, but it destroys our bodies. The body doesn't need excess sugar (other than what is found in fruits and vegetables), and we should never consume corn syrup. It is possible to give up sugar and have delicious food. Why not explore healthy, sugar-free alternatives?

Our home has a "no sugar" policy, but we still eat organic dark chocolate, bake with stevia, make our bread with almond flour, and make our pizza with a cauliflower crust. We are not deprived of anything; we cook differently.

The health benefits of lowering your sugar consumption are truly amazing!

Sugar – The Poison We Don't Talk About

Chapter 9
Hydration

What to drink and what not to drink.

Hydration is essential for our body's survival. We can go without food for weeks if we are hydrated. However, the human body will die within 3-5 days without water/hydration. Our bodies require water for the proper functioning of every cell.

Any liquid we intake will hydrate us, but not all drinks are equal. In fact, some will dehydrate us! This chapter will dive deep into what we drink and how it benefits our bodies. Let's start with the best drink we can have daily: water.

Water

Water forms the basis of blood, digestive juices, urine, sweat, feces, and tears. Water is also found in our muscles, fat, brain (85% water), and bones. Unlike camels, our bodies don't store water; therefore, we require fresh water daily. Water brings nutrients to cells, eliminating waste and protecting our joints and organs. It is used to keep our body temperature in homeostasis. You would never think of driving your car without water; it would overheat. Similarly, you should not expect your body to function correctly without hydration.

How Much Water Does the Human Body Require Daily?

The quantity of water we require daily varies from person to person. There are many variables, such as age, height, weight, sex, activity level, and even your climate. However, listed below is a general guide to follow from the Institute of Medicine (US):

- Men: Up to 13 cups (3 liters) daily.
- Women: Up to 9 cups (2+ liters) daily.
- Pregnant women: Up to 10 cups (2.36 liters) daily.
- Breastfeeding women: Up to 12 cups (2.83 liters) daily.
- Kids/teens: Up to 6-8 cups (1.41-1.89 liters) daily.
- Elderly: Up to 8 cups (1.89 liters) daily.

Note: We also get some water from eating fresh fruits and vegetables, which contributes to our hydration but should not take away from our daily natural water intake.

Are you dehydrated?

We can become dehydrated when we do not drink enough or lose more fluid than we take in. The severity of dehydration depends on many factors: whether it is a hot climate, whether you are working out, and what you are eating. You should drink before you are thirsty. Once you feel thirsty, you are already dehydrated. Your body shouldn't have to beg you for water; you should sip it all day.

Signs of dehydration:

Here are the typical signs of dehydration:

- Thirst
- Dry and sticky mouth
- Lack of urination
- Constipation
- Headache
- Foggy thinking
- Dark yellow urine
- Muscle cramps
- Dry, cool skin.

How to tell if you are over-hydrated? (Hyponatremia)

It is possible to over-hydrate. This can occur by drinking too much water over a full day or drinking too much water at one time. It will stress out your heart and kidneys; it can also damage the brain, leading to a potentially fatal outcome. Signs of hyponatremia include:

- Nausea
- Vomiting
- Headache
- Confusion
- Energy loss
- Fatigue
- Drowsiness
- Restlessness

- Irritability
- Muscle cramps (Weakness and spasms)
- Seizures
- Coma
- Heart Failure

Note: It is important not to drink all your water at one time. Start with some water when you first wake up. Throughout the day, drink sips of water regularly. Remember, if it is hot or you are working out, try to drink a little more.

There is a variety of water sources, and I am going to lay out some of the most popular ones and their pros and cons.

Tap Water

Tap water is the water that runs freely from a faucet.

Pros: Most tap water is safe to drink across much of Canada and the USA. Tap water isn't only good for you, but it's free and cheaper than buying water. It's also friendlier for the environment.

Cons: While there are set industry standards in place, there have been examples of harmful substances that may have somehow leaked into water supplies (e.g., pesticide residue, aluminum, hormones, and medications). However, this is often a one-off; there have been other examples, such as Flint, Michigan, etc. If you are concerned that the treatments performed on your water supply are sub-standard, then purchase a well-established home filtration system.

Mineral Water

Mineral water is water that is gathered from a mineral spring. This water contains minerals your body requires, such as magnesium and calcium.

Pros: Mineral water does have some health benefits. It provides minerals that your body can't make on its own. It can also aid with digestion. Mineral water tends to taste better than tap water.

Cons: One of the drawbacks to mineral water is the cost. Those who can't afford mineral water can purchase "trace minerals" from a health food store and add them to your filtered tap water.

Spring/Glacier Water

Spring or glacier water is bottled water that claims to be bottled directly from either a spring or glacier.

Pros: Spring or glacier water should be relatively clean and free from toxins while also containing minerals. Evian and Eska are two famous brand names; both are sold in stores everywhere.

Cons: Spring water is expensive, especially when compared to tap water. Also, some spring water is unfiltered and untested, posing potential health risks. In an article published in the Los Angeles Times by David Lazarus (Sept. 28, 2021), titled "You do know that, in most cases, bottled water is just tap water?" he exposes the fact that just because "spring water" claims to be from a spring or glacier does not mean it is. Some companies have even been caught selling tap water labeled "spring water."

Sparkling Water

Sparkling water is also referred to as carbonated water or soda water. Sparkling water (e.g., Bubly, Perrier, and San Pellegrino) is infused with carbon dioxide gas under pressure. This gives it a bubbly taste.

Pros: Sparkling water gives your mouth a taste of fizzy pop without all the sugar and additives. Having said that, some flavored sparkling waters contain sweeteners, and others with natural flavors. The bonus is that sparkling water is mineralized.

Cons: While there are some minerals in sparkling water, they are only trace amounts. Another drawback is the cost; some can be expensive. Some may also contain sugar, so read your labels.

Distilled Water

This type of water is boiled, and the steam is collected and condensed into liquid.

Pros: Distilled water is what you want to drink if you go to a foreign land or somewhere where the water may be unsafe. It is basically "dead water."

Cons: Distilled water contains no minerals. Therefore, there are no health benefits. In fact, any non-mineral water is dead water. So, again, add some trace minerals to this type of water.

Purified Water

Purified water is usually tap or groundwater that has been treated, removing harmful substances like bacteria, fungi, and parasites. This water is safe to consume.

Pros: Purified water is generally safe to drink.

Cons: Since all potentially harmful substances are removed from purified water, you also miss the mineral benefits. Once again, add your trace minerals to it.

Flavored Water (aka infused water)

Flavored water is sweetened with sugar, artificial sweeteners, and natural or artificial flavorings.

Pros: Flavored water offers a tastier alternative to plain water, making it easier to drink. You can add it to your regular water intake.

Cons: Sometimes, flavored water contains added sugar or artificial sweeteners, so read the labels carefully.

Alkaline Water

Alkaline water has a higher pH level than regular tap water. It also contains alkaline minerals and negative oxidation-reduction potential (ORP).

Pros: The fact that this type of water has a higher pH level has led some people to believe that it will neutralize acid in the body. The theory is that this would help slow aging and prevent cancer. However, this has not been scientifically proven.

Cons: Although it is safe to drink alkaline water, it can cause a reduction in stomach acid, which is not a good thing! If your stomach acid is too low, it fails to break down food properly, causing malabsorption (your stomach acid should be high 1.5-3.5). Lowering your stomach acid also lowers its ability to kill harmful bacteria.

Well Water

Well water comes from a hole dug deep into the

ground. The hole reaches groundwater from an aquifer (a layer of water-bearing rock or sediment) located very deep in the ground. This groundwater is the well water supply. The water is then drawn up to homes using a pump.

Pros: The convenience of well water is that it is easy to access.

Cons: While many use this raw, untreated water, there are potential risks. You should have your well tested regularly for bacteria, nitrates, and pH levels because there's potential contamination, especially from bacterial and parasitic infections like giardia. You don't know what you're getting until you test or treat the well water. I would recommend installing a filtration system.

Hydrogen Water

Hydrogen water is made by putting pure hydrogen gas into water. This can be done using electrolysis, which decomposes the water molecule into hydrogen and oxygen gas. This is a relatively new source, and many types of hydrogen water machines are available.

Pros: The claims for hydrogen water are that it decreases inflammation, boosts energy levels, and slows aging.

Cons: Research is being conducted on hydrogen water, but nothing is conclusive. The other con is the cost; hydrogen water machines can be costly.

Regular Teas

There is a wide variety of regular teas (e.g., black, green, chamomile, jasmine, etc.). Various types of regular tea are great liquids that increase attention and focus, protect the heart, improve gut health, and help to keep blood sugar levels stable. Green tea, specifically, is fantastic for skin and brain function, digestive relief, and headache prevention, and it can contribute to weight loss when consumed alongside a whole-food diet. Black teas, however, may be aggravating for those with stomach issues and caffeine sensitivities.

Herbal Teas

Drinking herbal teas is an easy and healthy way to hydrate your body! An endless variety of herbal teas can both hydrate and contribute to your overall health plan. Sugar-free, natural (organic) herbal tea is always a gold-star option! There are only pros for herbal teas.

Coffee

Over the years, we have heard about the many benefits of coffee. On the other hand, we have also heard reports vilifying coffee. There is enough information about the types of coffee beans, where they are from, and the wide variety of coffee drinks to fill an entire book. For this section, I will skim over coffee's basic pros and cons. My apologies to all the coffee aficionados who got excited when they saw the word “coffee.”

Where do I stand as a nutritionist in the coffee debate? I will answer that while sipping on my morning coffee. Yes, I love my coffee, and there is a wide variety of benefits to drinking it, but it is not for everyone.

Some Main Types of Coffee

Espresso

Espresso is Italian coffee. It’s brewed at high temperatures (close to boiling). The water is then pressurized and runs through finely grounded coffee beans. This coffee is dense and more concentrated than filter coffee. It’s served in “little cup” portions.

Filtered Coffee

Filter coffee is your drip coffee. It is a popular method of coffee brewing that extracts rich flavors from ground coffee via a paper or metal filter.

Percolated Coffee

This is coffee brewed in a coffee percolator. Boiling water is recirculated through the grounds repeatedly until it gets stronger and the coffee starts to boil. This means the coffee is consistently reheated and continually splashes over the coffee grounds in small bursts. This process sometimes makes the coffee taste bitter.

Instant Coffee

Instant coffee is derived from real coffee beans. The processing involves the extraction of the soluble and volatile properties of the beans. The water is then removed so only the concentrated soluble coffee powder remains. It's essentially been dehydrated for our convenience.

Keurig Coffee Machines (using coffee pods)

The Keurig coffee machine is a beverage brewing system that can be used at home or in your business. The machine uses individual coffee-filled pods to provide a single serving of coffee. These machines are rapid and convenient.

Iced Coffee

Iced coffee is a cold coffee beverage. It is usually prepared in one of two ways: by brewing coffee normally and pouring it over ice or cold milk or by brewing the coffee cold. Sugar, sweeteners, and flavoring can be added before cooling the hot coffee, making it a sweet drink.

Canned Coffee Drinks (e.g., Starbucks Triple Shot Vanilla)

There are currently several new canned coffee drinks on the market. However, the vast majority are high in sugar and additives. While canned coffee generally retains some nutritional qualities coffee beans offer, it should be consumed minimally due to all the extra additives. It's highly processed and costly. For example, Starbucks has canned coffee drinks in stores (Starbucks Iced Espresso Classic Vanilla Latte). This product has 30 grams of sugar (7.5 tsp), so just one drink will have more sugar than is recommended daily.

*The canned coffee drink "Caveman Coffee Nitro Cold Brew" has far more health benefits, containing only coffee, water, and nitrogen.

Bullet Proof Coffee

Bulletproof coffee is a popular keto high-fat breakfast drink named after the coffee company that initially created it. It's also known as "butter" coffee. Bulletproof coffee is a beautiful mixture of freshly brewed coffee, grass-fed butter, and MCT oil whipped into a frothy morning drink. The mix of good fats and coffee gives you a significant energy boost and is very satiating as it will boost the leptin hormone. This is my go-to coffee treat when I am fasting.

Benefits of Coffee (1-3 cups a day)

Pros: Coffee is an energy booster and is well processed by the liver, giving it tremendous hepatic benefits. Coffee has been proven to add to longevity. It also helps balance blood sugar (if no sugar or syrups are added), protecting against type 2 diabetes. Coffee is heart-protective and is good for your brain due to its vasodilating effects. Coffee has been known to be somewhat protective against Parkinson's disease (research is still being conducted). In fact, coffee has even been shown to protect our DNA.

Cons: Coffee can worsen symptoms of IBS (Irritable Bowel Syndrome) as it stimulates the bowels. Coffee should not be consumed if you are dealing with high anxiety/nervousness. Coffee consumed later in the day may cause sleep difficulties. People with stomach issues, such as ulcers or GERD, should avoid coffee altogether. However, coffee does help those with ADHD to focus; I can attest to that.

In summary, coffee can be added as a healthy drink to a whole-food meal plan. I caution against sugary, store-bought, canned, or ultra-processed coffee products. Remember to keep your food as close to natural as possible.

Buy good quality coffee beans, prepare them yourself, and enjoy. If you purchase your coffee from a store, get fresh, real coffee and add your full-fat cream. Don't overconsume coffee; having more of a good thing is never a good idea. One to three cups a day is a great guideline. Don't start now if you have never drank coffee or dislike the taste. Herbal teas are very healthy and great tasting as well.

Pop/Sodas/Soft Drinks

We may call them different names, but pop/soda/soft drinks and fizzy drinks are all sweet drinks containing carbonated water, sugar, flavoring, and chemical additives. We know these are unhealthy, but they taste great on a hot summer's day. It is estimated that in North America, we consume approximately 154 liters of pop per capita yearly. This works out to 1 out of 5 people having at least one pop a day. That's a lot of sugary drinks.

The occasional pop or soda is not a problem. However, North Americans are abusing this substance at an alarming rate. I see children in middle and high school show up with a can of Coke, Pepsi, or Monster Energy drinks to wake them up. Many of these kids are already dealing with learning disabilities, and that pop is definitely not helping.

The other trend I see is people who are obese trying to lose weight but who are addicted to pop. Remember, sugar addiction is very real. Commercials and advertising companies inundate our society with their products, making them more challenging to avoid. We are putting people in tough situations.

We also see healthy people who feel that pop is a guilty pleasure they can consume because they are not overweight. Let me give you a reality check. Just because you are thin or fit does not mean that a high amount of added sugar can't affect your liver and pancreas. A medical term for this is “TOFI” (thin on the outside, fat on the inside). You may appear fit or thin, but all that excess sugar and chemicals will still cause visceral fat around your internal organs, eventually leading to various diseases. I frequently see thin and fit people who are surprised when their doctor tells them they are pre-diabetic, diabetic, have NAFLD (non-alcoholic fatty liver disease), or even heart disease. We all need to care for our health, regardless of our size.

Is Diet Pop a Better Alternative?

While sugar-free is still not the healthiest choice, it can occasionally be added to your health plan. Diet pop has more additives and more chemicals, making it ultra-processed. There is no problem having an occasional diet pop, especially if your choices are sugary and diet pop. However, these should not be consumed daily.

Cons: Diet Pop contains no essential nutrients. They are entirely void of vitamins and minerals. Excessive amounts of diet drinks can cause gut health issues, erode tooth enamel, cause headaches, decrease bone density, and increase sugar cravings, leading to weight gain.

Store-bought Juices and Juicing

In 2013, a study published in the British Medical Journal found that there are benefits to eating fruit but not many benefits to drinking juice. Over 200,000 individuals were followed for twenty years while their diets were tracked. The results were conclusive: those who ate two servings a day of whole fruit reduced their risk of developing type 2 diabetes by 23%. The research found that apples, blueberries, and grapes were the best at lowering negative health risks like type 2 diabetes. The alarming discovery was that those who consumed one glass of juice per day (whether juiced at home or store-bought juice) increased their risk of developing diabetes by 21%.

This research summarized that eating two portions of whole fruits (especially berries) daily reduces your chances of developing diabetes. However, juicing or drinking your fruit (which tears up the fiber and increases the sugar content) will increase your chance of developing type 2 diabetes. Why? Because drinking sugary fruit juice (even reduced sugar or freshly juiced fruit) will spike your blood sugar/insulin levels. The raised blood sugar levels can affect your liver, pancreas, and, eventually, the heart.

Now, for the average healthy and active person (especially active children), you should enjoy three servings of whole fresh fruit a day but avoid juicing. This way, you get the best nutrients out of your fruit; the gut loves that fiber, and it will decrease the sugar transit time.

Alcohol

The National Institute on Alcohol Abuse and Alcoholism (NIAA) recommends no more than one drink per day for women or two drinks a day for men. Now remember one drink is equal to 4 oz of wine, one beer, or 1 oz of hard liquor. More than that, the liver is going to become compromised. So, if you enjoy a four oz glass of wine with your supper, you will be fine, and there may even be some health benefits. The trouble is most people have a few drinks a night. What is worse, some people don't drink during the week and then binge drink over the weekend. Either way, alcohol is a toxin to the body. The liver can process it, but just like sugar, it cannot be processed in large quantities. It's also not as "beneficial" for us as was originally thought. Much of the new research is showing us there are no real health benefits of alcohol. So, if it is habit-forming and difficult for the liver to process, perhaps it is not the best drink to consume on a regular basis.

Alcohol will stall weight loss. When the liver receives alcohol, it will process the alcohol first because it is recognized as a poison (much like sugar). While the liver is struggling to metabolize the alcohol, it is not processing fats. The priority for your body will be to get rid of the alcohol, and your fat-burning will take a back burner.

Alcohol also dehydrates your body and can cause bloating, weight gain, and skin issues. Long-term effects of alcohol include high blood pressure, heart disease, stroke, liver disease, and digestive problems. Alcohol is also linked to breast cancer, mouth, and throat cancer, esophageal cancer, cancer of the voice box, liver cancer, colon cancer, and rectal cancer. Alcoholism and alcohol dependency not only destroy your body, but they can also destroy your relationships. I always ask patients, "What is your relationship with alcohol? Do you control alcohol, or does alcohol control you?" This is an important question for all of us.

To summarize, alcohol in small amounts is doable. The health issues with alcohol come with larger amounts (more than one drink a day for women and two drinks a day for men) or weekend binge drinking. That hangover you are dealing with after drinking is your body responding to being poisoned. Your body is desperately trying to purge itself of toxins that are harming you. Alcohol also lowers your inhibitions and makes you eat more because you end up craving sugar and carbohydrates. Sugary alcoholic beverages contain a lot of extra calories, ultimately leading to weight gain.

I am often asked where I stand on alcohol personally. I am going to be very vulnerable at this point and share my personal story on alcohol. In the past, I enjoyed my evening ritual of drinking a glass of dry red wine. I felt it was healthier for me as it was low in carbohydrates. I also believed the resveratrol in the red wine would have some great health benefits for me. I would always have my glass of red wine with a plate of cheese. It was my favorite time of day.

A few years later, I went from one glass of red wine a night to two. Eventually, I was drinking three glasses a night. I was gaining a bit of weight and had a constant low-grade headache. My mind was foggy, and I noticed a puffiness on my face. I was becoming a little too dependent on my nightly "red wine ritual." I knew I was not an alcoholic because I would go long periods without wine (dry January and November). Still, I did notice I no longer had a healthy relationship with alcohol.

When my mother was diagnosed with Alzheimer's, I became her overseer, and it broke my heart. She was slowly losing her memories, and we were watching it happen. That made me re-evaluate my own life and health choices. At that time, one of my daughters began sending me articles on the link between alcohol use and Alzheimer's; she did not want to see me lose my memories like her grandmother. That did it! I decided to stop drinking cold turkey.

I let everyone in my life know that I was choosing to stop drinking so that they would hold me accountable. I then replaced my nightly "red wine ritual" with a new ritual. I would pour sparkling water into a nice glass and take a bubble bath in the evening. This would be my new "evening reward ." The first month was a challenge trying to swap this reward system; I missed my wine! However, after the first month, I reset the habit and began to feel much better! My face thinned out, I was losing weight again, my brain fog started lifting, and I was thinking clearer. I also noticed I was sleeping better and was much calmer in general. My weight-lifting workouts also improved as I had more energy! By the third month of being alcohol-free, I decided never to go back, and I severed my relationship with alcohol.

Today, I buy non-alcoholic dry red wine when invited to functions with alcohol, or I have soda water with lime. This way, no one feels awkward around me, and I feel like I am joining in. However, I'm finding more and more people I meet have also given up alcohol. I conclude by saying that you can get your resveratrol from grapes, blueberries, raspberries, and mulberries!

Energy Drinks

Energy drinks contain large amounts of sugar ranging from 21g to 34g (5.25 to 8.5 tsp). The main types of sugar are sucrose, glucose, and high fructose corn syrup. There are also many additives in energy drinks that can over-tax the body. This is why regular consumption of energy drinks increases the risk of obesity, insulin resistance, metabolic syndrome, and type 2 diabetes.

Here is a list of just some of the side effects of regularly consuming energy drinks:

- Dehydration
- Intestinal bacteria disruption
- Heart palpitations
- Anxiety/jitters
- Muscle twitching
- Stomach upset
- Headaches
- Restlessness
- An energy crash follows a massive burst of energy once the side effects wear off.

I don't recommend energy drinks to anyone, especially children or youth. If you need to occasionally consume an energy drink (e.g., truck drivers), purchase sugar-free or zero-sugar products. Just remember to consume them very sparingly.

Summary of Chapter 9

Hydration is vital to the human body. We can only survive 3-5 days without water, so we must stay hydrated throughout the day.

1. Water: Water forms the basis of blood, our digestive juices, urine, sweat, feces, and tears. Water makes up every cell and is required for our muscles, fat, brain, and bones. Some water is safer and has more benefits than others.
2. Teas and herbal teas: A wide variety of regular and herbal teas exist. There are health benefits to each.
3. Coffee: Coffee is an energy booster and is well processed by the liver, giving it tremendous hepatic benefits. Coffee has been proven to have many health benefits and may add to longevity.
4. Pops/soda/soft drinks: There is a wide variety of pops containing sugar, carbonated water, flavoring, and chemical additives. The occasional pop won't harm you, but drinking it regularly will have a negative effect on your body. When you feel the need to have a pop, try sparkling water. None of these drinks (regular or diet) contribute to your health.
5. Juices and juicing: Eat two to three portions of whole fruits daily and skip the juices or fruit smoothies. Whole fruit has far more health benefits than juice.

6. Alcohol: The National Institute on Alcohol Abuse and Alcoholism (NIAA) recommends no more than one drink per day for women and no more than two drinks per day for men. One drink equals 4 oz of wine, one beer, or 1 oz of hard liquor. New research shows us there are no real health benefits of alcohol. So, if it is habit-forming and challenging for the liver to process, perhaps it is best not to consume alcohol.

7. Energy drinks: Energy drinks contain large amounts of sugar ranging from 21 g to 34 g (5.25 to 8.5 tsp). They also contain additives that can over-tax the body. Regular consumption of energy drinks increases the risk of obesity, insulin resistance, metabolic syndrome, and type 2 diabetes. Children, youth, or people with anxiety, heart issues, diabetes, or metabolic issues should never consume energy drinks.

Hydration – What to Drink and What Not to Drink

Chapter 10
Baby to Preteen Nutrition

What to Feed Your Child

Introduction

Proper food can set your baby up for success! As a mom, you have gone to great lengths to grow a wonderful human for nine months. You have successfully brought a beautiful gift into the world, and this is just the beginning. What you will feed that baby right now will determine its nutritional health for life. We don't want our babies to "only" feel full; we want them to get every nutrient needed to build a healthy body and mind as they grow into adulthood. A child starved of various nutrients is going to be a sick adult and, in turn, a very ill senior. With all the new nutritional research we currently have, we definitely know what to feed our babies, toddlers, and children. Excellent nutrition as babies will nourish their bodies, brains, and immune systems for life. Also, starting babies and toddlers on a clean, whole-food diet will help them develop their taste buds for good food. Once you give babies and toddlers poor-quality processed foods, their taste buds will change. It becomes difficult once they desire sugary, poor-quality food over healthy whole foods. It is far easier to start them off with whole foods young, and you will see them crave vegetables, fruit, and various meats as they grow. Set your baby up for true nutritional success; it's easier than you think!

Breast is Best, But Fed is Nutritionally Friendly

The breastfeeding versus bottle feeding debate has been going on for decades. We have some extreme zealots on each side who would argue their points well. However, as a nutritionist, I see things a little differently. Your baby needs to be fed well. They need a mom who loves them and gives them the nutrition they require to grow properly. Both breastfeeding and bottle feeding (depending on what is in the bottle) can provide that. I breastfed all of my children for about 18 months. That worked for me. They gained weight and were healthy babies. However, around that same time, I knew other women who could not breastfeed. One of them was a mom who had adopted a new infant. All of their babies also gained weight and were very healthy. We must not shame or blame those who can't breastfeed; it's time for women to learn to be kind and supportive of other mothers. The critical factors to an infant's well-being are:

- Love
- Safety
- Excellent nutrition.

So, I strongly suggest we present a case for good health and help the mother beside us become a success in her own way.

Breast Feeding Benefits

Breast milk is meant to be the highest form of nutrition for an infant. It contains all three macro-nutrients: fats, carbohydrates, and protein. Breastmilk also has all the nutrients required for your baby's body, brain, and nervous system to thrive. The colostrum that the mother produces before the milk comes in is the building block for the baby's immune system. Breast milk provides a unique formulation of vitamins, minerals, and antioxidants. It is also easier for an infant's stomach and intestines to absorb and digest nutrients. The colostrum contains antibodies that protect against infection and boost the baby's immune system.

Breastfeeding has many benefits for the mother's body and mind. One is the bonding that occurs as the mother feeds her child. Breastfeeding helps the woman's body repair and return to its natural state. Did you know that when a mother breastfeeds her child, the hormones "prolactin and oxytocin" are released? While prolactin is the hormone that makes breast milk, oxytocin works hard to repair the mother. Oxytocin contracts the uterus during breastfeeding to aid in stopping the bleeding. When the baby is suckling, the uterus contracts, helping it return to its original state. This hormone also has a built-in calming effect on the mother.

Mothers' Health Matters

The food the breastfeeding mother eats is a game

changer. The mother's milk may be less than optimal for the baby if the mother is severely nutrient deficient, consumes excessive junk food or sugar, smokes/vapes, consumes alcohol, or is on drugs. Some diseases may be passed through breast milk, such as HIV (if viral load is high), Hepatitis B, Hepatitis C, West Nile Virus, cytomegalovirus, and HTLV ½ (human T-cell lymphotropic virus). In summary, if the mother is healthy and eats a proper whole-food diet, her baby will thrive.

Baby Formula

Commercial formulas have had some issues. Over the years, there have been concerns over baby formulas. A recent example was a recall of Similac, EleCare, and Alimentum powdered infant formula in February 2022. After investigating these products (produced at Abbott Nutrition's Sturgis facility in Michigan, USA), the FDA found they contained a bacterium called Cronobacter. The symptoms of being affected by Cronobacter include fever, difficulty feeding, excessive crying, fatigue, and seizures in rare cases. This recall was a wake-up call to mothers everywhere. We don't always know what is in these products; we are expected to trust manufacturers blindly.

So, what do we do if we need to feed our infants and the breast is not an option? Look for organic powdered formula made with a goat's milk base (if possible). Goat milk has more health benefits than cow's milk and is easier to digest. Compared to cow's milk, goat milk has a higher level of αS2-casein. AS2-casein forms smaller flocs of aggregated protein that infants can digest more effectively. The better the digestion, the more nutrients are absorbed, making your baby healthier.

When you are purchasing powdered infant formula, read the label. Here are some things you should avoid in baby formula:

Faux Iron

Faux iron is added to many infant formulas. However, faux iron does not actually add iron to the product. It is an electrolyte found as a fortified powder. The problem with regular consumption of faux iron is that it can cause digestive issues. Some studies show that long-term consumption can also lead to future cardiovascular problems.

High Fructose Corn Syrup

High-fructose corn syrup (HFCS) should always be avoided, especially for infants. It is a poor-quality sweetener that the liver has difficulty processing. A diet high in HFCS may set an infant up for insulin issues, which may lead to obesity, diabetes, and liver issues later on in life. High fructose corn syrup is added to many infant formulas because it is cheap. Yes, it is inexpensive, but it is far from healthy!

Poor Quality Oils

Poor-quality oils are often found in formulas, so avoid infant formula made with vegetable oil, canola oil, rapeseed oil, or corn oil. These oils are added to infant formula because they are cheaper to use than actual cow's milk fat or goat milk fat. These cheap-quality oils can cause malabsorption, diarrhea, and dehydration.

Preservatives

Preservatives are sometimes listed in the ingredients of baby formula. These may be listed under "sulfur dioxide" or "additives." These can cause digestive issues in infants.

Rice Powder-Based Infant Formula

Rice powder-based infant formula contains low levels of arsenic and is a poor-quality protein. Rice is used simply because it is cheaper to make the product.

Soy-Based Infant Formula

Soy-based infant formula should also be avoided. Infants fed soy are more likely to develop osteopenia, the weakening of bones. Bones would receive far more calcium from formula made from cow's or goat's milk as a base. Soy also has a higher presence of aluminum. Aluminum may affect bone growth and the central nervous system.

I would advise you to find a product with goat milk as the foundation. There is a company in New Zealand called "Little Oak" that ships directly to Canada. They make products for infants and toddlers and appear reputable and well-recommended in New Zealand. It's pricey, but your child will thank you for it.

I have met some mothers who have made their baby formulas successfully. However, Health Canada and the Pediatric Society of Canada advise against this practice because it is not overseen or regulated.

In conclusion, I will always suggest breastfeeding if at all possible. It is both the best and cheapest option. However, I will stress that what the mother eats and her overall health plays a vital part in the success of her baby's well-being. For those who can't breastfeed, choose the very best formula you can and focus on loving your baby!

Cereal/Pablum

The problem with whole-grain cereal.

Today's grains are difficult to digest; this is true for adults, especially babies with young digestive systems. Grains carry phytic acid (we discussed this in the grain chapter). Phytic acid hinders the absorption of minerals like iron and calcium, vital nutritional components for your baby's health.

Our ancestors could feed their babies grain and rice cereals because, at that time, grains were not grown with harsh pesticides. The grain was grown in nutritionally dense soil, and GMOs were not yet considered. The rice and grains we consume today are not the same as our great-grandparents ate.

If you introduce grains as a part of your baby's diet, prepare them yourself, and don't trust commercial brands. Commercial foods are there to make a profit. I suggest preparing your grains by soaking, sprouting, or fermenting them prior to use. This will increase nutrient absorption and will make them more easily digestible.

The problem with rice cereal.

I don't ever recommend rice cereals for babies because rice contains low levels of arsenic. Arsenic is also found in other foods; however, of the 19% of arsenic exposures in babies aged 4-24 months, rice cereal accounted for 55%. It is not suitable for adults and definitely not good for children. Arsenic is a real issue when it comes to rice. It is found in our soil due to pesticides that are sprayed to increase our crops. Rice is one of those plants that absorbs toxins very quickly and easily. All plants can absorb toxins, but rice soaks it up more due to the water environment in which it grows. I am amazed that there are currently no regulations regarding the arsenic concentrations in food (including infant rice cereal) within Canada and the US. Europe has much stricter regulations!

Many newer studies have proven that arsenic exposure in rice cereal exceeds the US Environmental Protection Agency's maximum contaminant levels and evidently increases arsenic exposure among babies.

Excellent Baby Cereal Options

I would suggest three baby cereal types that have proven far healthier than the average rice cereal. These would be quinoa-based baby cereals, almond-based baby cereal, and buckwheat-based cereal. The baby food company "Else" carries many of these products. Their products are available on Iherb.com.

Note: Add a pureed fruit (like bananas, cooked apples, or cooked blueberries) to make it tasty and increase the nutrient value.

Introducing Foods

By six months, babies can begin consuming pureed/mashed foods. I recommend delaying more solid food until they can sit up independently, support their head/body, and start to reach for food. So, what should we feed them to set them up for excellent health?

Here is a list of some foods you can begin to add in. Remember to start with pureed form, then gradually progress to mashed, then finger food.

- Sweet potato
- Squash
- Peas
- Carrots
- Banana
- Avocado
- Green beans
- Meats (beef, chicken, turkey, salmon)

Around seven months, you can begin moving from pureed to mashed. At that time, you can also introduce mashed scrambled eggs with grass-fed butter or MCT oil, plain full-fat yogurt with mashed fruit, and full-fat cheeses. You can also introduce organic nut butter into the yogurt or cereal.

I strongly suggest you make your baby food; it is ridiculously easy, far cheaper, and safer than jarred baby food. Back then, I fed all of my babies whatever we were eating. If we were having roast beef, mashed potatoes, and peas, I would blend a small amount with some of the beef broth until it was pureed. They loved it. I would mash up bananas and cook blueberries and apples. I then blended them and made my own pureed fruit. My babies ate very well, and they loved the homemade foods.

When trying to save time, I would pre-make their baby food, put it in ice cube trays, and freeze the food. Once frozen, I would put them in air-tight bags, label and date them, and keep them in the freezer until I needed them. I would then thaw them and heat them on the stove. You can blend and mix any whole food meat (poultry, pork, fish that is low in mercury) and any vegetable or fruit. Add a little meat juice and vegetable water to help make it a little more liquid-based. You would be so surprised at how much babies enjoy these foods. As a mother, you will not only feel good about feeding your baby quality foods but also know exactly what is in the food you're giving your child.

Note: By my third and fourth babies, I got pretty creative. I blended dinners like lasagna or shepherd's pie; the babies would go crazy over these two meals!

I would suggest starting babies on meats and vegetables first because once they taste that sweet fruit, their taste buds will always want it first.

I suggest scrambled eggs (organic/omega 3) as a starter breakfast. I would mash in a little grass-fed butter or MCT oil. You could also give them some blended beef or chicken liver. Another option is full-fat Greek yogurt (never low-fat) with mixed berries or bananas. Avoid adding extra sugar; the fruit is sweet enough for them.

Remember water. When introducing solids, always ensure you have a sippy cup or bottle with some water in it. Babies need to be hydrated, too.

What about milk? After 12 months, I would first add full-fat goat's milk, as it is easier to digest. By 18 months, try full-fat cow's milk (not 1%, 2%, or skim) and monitor their digestion and bowel movements. If they are adjusting well to it, then continue. If they get rashes, stomach cramping, or diarrhea, switch back to goat milk.

Growing up in a farming community, we had raw cow's milk from a very young age up to adulthood. We skipped the goat's milk because we couldn't access it. We all grew up healthy and "relatively well adjusted"!

Teething Foods

Infants can hold onto and suck on a variety of foods, like:

- Long slices of beef
- Carrot sticks
- Slices of avocado
- Whole green beans
- Snap peas
- Sliced pepper
- Long strips of cooked sweet potatoes

- Sliced fruits or berries
- Finger foods
- Sprouted grain or sourdough bread toasted and cut into strips with nut butter.

Try to avoid all the commercial "baby/toddler" snacks. They are ultra-processed and not the best choice.

Make Your Baby Teething Biscuits

Recipe from Superhealthykids.com (follow them for other great ideas)

Ingredients

- 2 cups oats – dry
- 1 medium banana
- 2 tablespoons coconut oil

Optional

- 1 teaspoon vanilla extract
- 1/8 teaspoon cinnamon

Instructions

- Preheat oven to 350 degrees.
- Prepare a baking sheet with parchment paper or a silicone baking mat.
- Blend the oats into a fine powder in a food processor (or blender).

- Add banana and coconut oil (and any vanilla or spices you may be using) to the blender and puree until the mixture comes together in a dough.
- If the dough is very sticky to handle, you can pat a little flour (gluten-free or wheat flour) onto the ball's exterior to make it easier to handle. If the dough is too dry, you can add a bit of additional coconut oil.
- Divide the dough into 12 balls or sections. Pat out each ball into a little baton about 4 inches long, 1 to 1 ½ inches wide, and about 1/4 inch thick. Round the edges of each baton with your fingers so there are no sharp edges.
- (Alternatively, you can roll the entire dough ball out into a rectangle about ¼ inch thick and slice it into 12 rectangles. Round the corners of each rectangle and make the shapes roughly even. I've found that shaping each baton works better for me than rolling and slicing, but you can do what works best for you).
- Place evenly on a baking sheet so none of the batons are touching. Bake at 350 degrees for 10 minutes. Flip and cook another 5-10 minutes until the edges are golden and the centers are set but not too crunchy.
- Allow to cool and store in an airtight container at room temperature, refrigerator, or freezer.

As They Grow

As your children grow, remember to keep it simple. Apply the 80/20 rule: 80 % of the time, have them eat whole foods (organic, fresh, or at least local when possible), healthy meats, vegetables, fruits, organic whole grains, nuts seeds, good oils (grass-fed butter, avocado oil, MCT oil, coconut oil, olive oil), home baked treats and the keep sugar to a minimum. The remaining 20% of the time is spent on special treats. Birthdays, holidays, movies, and fun events should be the 20% of the time to get whatever they would like (unless there are allergies or ADHD/Autism issues, which we will discuss below).

Keep their sugar under control by trying to encourage fruit and healthy snacks. You can bake and make yummy treats without all the processing. If you don't have junk food in the home, they won't eat it. If you start right from infancy, guiding your nutrition throughout the years will be easier. It's harder to draw them back to a whole foods diet after their taste buds have adjusted to junk food or ultra-processed foods, but it is possible. I have seen families make massive food changes and have seen it work.

ADHD, Autism AuDHD

Many kids today are being diagnosed with ADHD, autism, or a form of both (AuDHD). So, I thought adding the nutritional recommendations for both of these was essential. I know a lot about controlling ADHD through food instead of medication because I have ADHD.

I have learned to control my symptoms through regular exercise, proper sleep, and a whole-food, clean keto diet. The times I have had sugar or foods with a lot of additives, I can definitely spiral. At this age, I have learned to stick to my meal plan and enjoy my food and the well-being it provides.

What are ADHD, Autism, and AuDHD?

Autism Spectrum Disorder (ASD)

Autism Spectrum Disorder (ASD) is a complex developmental condition that involves challenges with social cues and communication, restricted interests, and repetitive behaviors. The five key signs of autism in children are as follows;

- Poor eye contact
- Reactions to light and sounds
- Particular and focused interests
- Repeating phrases or words
- Repetitive behaviors (tapping, leg shaking, picking skin, hair pulling, tongue clicking)
- Toe walking or walking in circles
- Delayed language development or non-verbal communication

- Intense reactions to small changes in routine or surroundings.

Autism can be a large spectrum, so you can have a child who is non-communicative or a child who is very high functioning and only struggles with social situations.

Attention Deficit Hyperactive Disorder (ADHD)

Attention-deficit/hyperactivity disorder (ADHD) is one of the most common disorders affecting children today. Symptoms of ADHD include inattention (not being able to keep focus), hyperactivity (excess movement), and impulsivity (acts that occur in the moment without thought).

The most common ADHD symptoms displayed in children are as follows:

- Difficulty sitting still (especially in quiet surroundings)
- Constantly fidgeting
- Unable to concentrate on tasks
- Excessive physical movement
- Excessive talking and interrupting
- Unable to take turns and act without thinking.

AuDHD is a relatively new term that describes kids/adults who have a combination of both autism and ADHD. Recent research estimates that 40-70% of autistic individuals also have a form of ADHD.

Some of the typical symptoms of AuDHD are as follows:

- Impulse control
- Learning difficulties
- Social difficulties
- Inattention,
- Emotional dysregulation
- Stimming (repetitive physical movements, sounds, or words that soothe them)
- Sensory challenges (to lights, sounds, smells or tastes, textures of touch)
- Difficulties with executive functions.

Treatments for ADHD, Autism, and AuDHD

Doctors will prescribe various pharmaceuticals and therapies for these neurotypes (Adderall, Dexedrine, Focalin, and Ritalin, to name a few). However, a lot can be done to control symptoms through lifestyle and nutrition. For the sake of this chapter, I will only focus on the nutritional aspect.

What to Avoid with Autism

Kids diagnosed with autism should avoid sugar, MSG, artificial ingredients, toxins, low-fat dairy (if there is a dairy allergy, remove it altogether), gluten, and corn.

What to Avoid With ADHD

Children diagnosed with ADHD should avoid sugar, pop, fast food, ultra-processed meals, processed snack foods, and artificial colors, especially red and yellow dyes. Also, avoid food additives like aspartame, MSG, sodium benzoate, and nitrites.

What to Eat With Either ADHD, Autism, or AuDHD

There are two solid ways of eating for children and adults who fall into the ADHD, Autism, or AuDHD camps.

The first diet I would suggest is called the Specific Carbohydrate Diet. This diet would be well suited for children (or adults) with autism or ADHD. This diet has also been successful for those who have asthma, allergies, or autoimmune disorders. These diseases have a common thread – they can be linked to gut issues. Those gut issues can cause food sensitivities and digestion issues, leading to nutrient malabsorption. A recent medical research study found that over 43% of autism patients developed "leaky gut syndrome." A leaky gut will lead to vitamin/mineral deficiencies, inflammation, and toxins in the bloodstream. Along with the Specific Carbohydrate Diet, it is very important to incorporate good sleep habits and regular exercise programs.

What Do You Eat on the Specific Carbohydrate Diet?

Animal Proteins to Eat

- Fresh or frozen beef
- Fresh or frozen lamb
- Fresh or frozen pork
- Fresh or frozen poultry
- Fresh or frozen fish
- Fresh or frozen shellfish
- Eggs
- Aged cheeses
- Homemade yogurt or full-fat yogurt

Animal Proteins to Avoid

- Processed meats and processed cheeses
- Hot dogs
- Bologna
- Turkey loaf
- Sliced ham
- Breaded fish
- Canned meats
- Processed cheese/cheese slices
- Cheeze Whiz

Vegetables and Legumes to Eat

- Artichoke (not Jerusalem)
- Asparagus
- Beets
- Dried white navy beans

- Lentils
- Split peas
- Broccoli
- Brussels sprouts
- Cabbage
- Cauliflower
- Carrots
- Celery
- Cucumbers
- Dill pickles
- Eggplant
- Kale
- Garlic
- All lettuce
- Lima beans
- Mushrooms
- Mustard greens
- Olives
- Onions
- Parsley
- Peas
- Pumpkin
- Spinach
- Winter/summer squash
- String beans
- Tomatoes
- Turnips
- Watercress

Not allowed: Any flours, germs, pasta, starches, or cereal products made from the list below:

- Canned vegetables
- White and sweet potatoes
- Corn
- Yams
- Parsnips
- Bean sprouts
- Soybean
- Mung beans
- Fava beans
- Garbanzo beans
- Amaranth flour
- Jerusalem artichoke flour/powder
- Quinoa
- Cottonseed
- Tapioca
- Sago
- Seaweed

Grains to Avoid

- Arrowroot
- Barley
- Buckwheat
- Bulgur
- Millet
- Oats
- Rice
- Rye
- Triticale
- Wheat

Fruits to Eat (Fresh, raw, frozen, or dried)

- Apples
- Avocados
- Apricots
- Ripe Bananas
- All Berries
- Cherries
- Coconut
- Grapefruit
- Grapes
- Kiwi
- Kumquats
- Lemons
- Limes
- Mangoes
- Melons
- Nectarines
- Oranges
- Papayas
- Peaches
- Pears
- Pineapples
- Prunes
- Raisins
- Rhubarb
- Tangerines

Not Allowed

- Canned fruits
- Sweetened dried fruit
- Molasses

- Ketchup (unless homemade)
- Agar-agar
- Jams and jellies

<u>Nuts to Eat</u>

- Almonds
- Brazil nuts
- Cashews and chestnuts
- Filberts
- Hazelnuts
- Pecans
- Walnuts

<u>Nuts to Avoid</u>

- Beer nuts
- Glazed nuts
- Roasted nuts/peanuts in salted mixtures

<u>Beverages to Drink</u>

- Tomato/vegetable juices
- Unsweetened fruit juices
- Weak tea or coffee
- Peppermint or spearmint herbal tea
- Milkshakes (made with homemade yogurt, fruit, and honey)
- Freshly squeezed vegetable or fruit juices made from the list of allowed foods

Do Not Drink

- Cow milk
- Goat milk
- Soy milk
- Rice milk
- Canned coconut milk
- Instant coffee or tea
- Coffee substitutes
- Soft drinks

The Specific Carbohydrate Diet has shown success and should be your first go-to meal plan. However, fruit juices, dried fruits, and grains may not work for all. For instance, some children (and adults) who failed on the SC diet found success on a Ketogenic diet. Children who deal with obesity, gluten allergies, celiac disease, or seizures have responded better to Keto. If one doesn't work, try the other, as both can be an effective tool.

Ketogenic Diet for ADHD, Autism, and AuDHD

Many families have found tremendous relief for their children struggling with the symptoms of ADHD and autism through a formatted Ketogenic diet. In June 2024, Loma Linda University (Loma Linda, California) published a review of "The Ketogenic Diet in the Treatment of Autism Spectrum Disorder" written by Eugene Reznik. At the end of the review, it was concluded that a Ketogenic diet was a helpful tool in controlling certain behaviors. See the conclusion below:

"The data suggests that implementation of a ketogenic diet improves core and associated psychiatric symptoms of autism spectrum disorder such as repetitive behaviors, social behaviors, communication, anxiety, speech, hyperactivity, and cognition."

In 2021, Pub Med Central published an article in the National Library of Medicine titled "A Ketogenic Diet and the Treatment of Autism Spectrum Disorder." While the research paper concludes that there was success with the Ketogenic diet, it was hard for some children to follow, especially those with very picky food choices. The keto diet did help control behaviors similar to those mentioned in the above review. Below is a clip from the conclusion of the research paper:

"A Ketogenic Diet may improve social behavior in ASD via normalizing GABA, improving mitochondrial function, ameliorating inflammatory activity and oxidative stress in the brain, inhibiting the mTOR signaling pathway, and modulating the gut microbiota. However, the effects of KD vary widely between ASD patients, and the underlying mechanisms are not known. ASD children may also reject KD food because of their selective eating habits, which complicates the introduction of a KD to ASD patients." See the citation in the bibliography.

Some families I have worked with have had success with the keto diet, while others have had success with the carbohydrate-specific diet. It is really a situation of trial and error. I know a few families who have also seen improvements in focus and behaviors by removing sugar, fructose, and ultra-processed foods. If you want to try the ketogenic diet for ADHD and autism, go to the chapter “The Best Diets,” where you will find the food layout for the Ketogenic diet.

Vitamin D and Zinc Deficiency

Vitamin D and Zinc deficiency linked to autism and ADHD have been shown to be an issue. Children with ASD, ADHD, and AuDHD consistently report significantly lower vitamin D (and zinc) levels than those of neurotypical children. For this reason, I would strongly advise parents to see a physician or naturopath who would conduct a vitamin/mineral deficiency test. Food and supplements could make a real difference.

Summary of Chapter 10

Nutrition is our health's foundation and a vital key to raising healthy children. What we feed our babies, toddlers, and growing children can have significant health implications for the future. As parents, we must take the time to set the next generation up for success when it comes to health!

1. We spoke about breastfeeding being the best nutrition for infants, but there are healthy choices if you can't breastfeed.
2. I explained the difficulties with commercial pablum and baby cereal and how to find healthier choices
3. In the section on first foods, we discussed some great alternatives on how to make your own purees, mashed food, and early starter meals.
4. As your child grows, we discussed how a whole-food diet is best. The foundation of your child's nutritional plan should be real food prepared and cooked at home. We also discussed the 80/20 rule: eat healthy 80% of the time, and the remaining 20% is for your treats and junk foods.
5. We discussed the differences between ADHD, autism, and AuDHD and what the key symptoms are for each.
6. In the final section, we covered the different types of diets for those dealing with these neurotypes. I spoke about three recommended diets: carb-specific, Ketogenic, and a basic whole foods diet free from sugar and ultra-processed foods. I also mentioned the need for vitamin deficiency testing to check for Vitamin D and Zinc deficiencies.

Takeaway from Chapter 10

Our job as parents is vital, and one of the best things you can do throughout your child's life is to feed them a healthy diet. A healthy foundation sets them up for healthy adulthood. I would go one step further and say be the example of how to live healthy –children learn more from what they see than what they are told.

Baby to Pre-teen Nutrition

Chapter 11
How Food Affects Hormones and Organs

Back in the day, we used the phrase "a calorie is a calorie." Today, research shows that this is far from the truth. Here is one example: you eat a 10 oz steak, which is equivalent to 615 calories, or you can eat a 1.5 pkg of chocolate-covered Oreos (also 615 calories). Are you saying that once absorbed by the body, the calories react with your hormones and organs the same way? If so, it doesn't matter which food you eat as long as you stay within a specific calorie limit. That is not possible. Quality matters.

Science has repeatedly proven that food is vitally important because it is metabolized differently depending on its nutrient values. Our body is intelligent; it knows what to do with the real whole foods we consume. On the other hand, when we ingest highly processed foods that contain sugar, poor-quality oils, additives, and chemicals, it takes our organs a lot of work to process and affects various hormones.

In the above scenario, the steak will be processed quickly by the body and is far more nutrient-dense. The liver will process it without any difficulty. That steak will come close to meeting your daily requirement for heme iron and B12. It will turn on the leptin hormone, making you feel full.

It will also not spike your insulin levels.

Compare that to the Oreos, which are loaded with trans fats, sugar, and additives. They have zero nutrient value, and the sugar and trans fats will be difficult for the liver to process. What about your pancreas? Those Oreos will drastically spike your insulin and turn on the Ghrelin hormone, making you again hungry for more sugar or maybe a sweet drink. That is the simple biology of food metabolism.

The way the organs and hormones interact with food will determine your health. The hormones activated by food will affect your hunger, energy, and even mental health. A calorie is *not* just a calorie. That is why most people trying to lose weight by counting calories fail. I want to change that for you. I believe knowledge is power, and people don't fail because of a lack of willpower; they fail because of a lack of knowledge. You will want to eat healthier when you study your body, how it works, and how your food impacts it. That is the knowledge I want you to have.

Let's start with a little refresher on how our body processes food.

Our bodies are wonderfully made, and each step of the digestive system is calculated. Your food moves through your gastrointestinal (GI) tract via peristalsis. The hollow organs of your GI tract (from mouth to anus) contain a layer of muscle that enables their walls to move the food along.

The pulsing movement pushes your food and liquid through your GI tract and then mixes with the juices of each organ. The muscle behind the food contracts and squeezes, continually pushing the food forward. The muscle in front of the food relaxes; this allows the food to move along smoothly.

We begin this process when we put food in our mouths. As our teeth chew and tear the food, enzymes are released to break down the food. That is why it is so important to "eat your food" instead of drinking it. Those enzymes released will break the food down to increase the nutrient value you will eventually absorb. The food then starts to move through your GI tract. When you swallow, your tongue pushes the food into your throat. The epiglottis (a small piece of tissue) then folds over your windpipe to prevent you from choking.

Once you begin swallowing, the process becomes automatic. Your brain signals the muscles of the esophagus to start working, and that is when peristalsis (wave-like movements) happen. Once the food reaches the lower esophagus sphincter, it relaxes and lets it drop into your stomach. This sphincter stays closed to keep what's in your stomach from flowing back into your esophagus.

Note: GERD (gastroesophageal disease) is where the stomach contents flow back into your esophagus.

Once in the stomach, the stomach muscles churn the food and liquid with your stomach acids to break down the food and release the nutrients. The stomach slowly empties its contents into your small intestine. The product passed by the stomach to the intestines is called "chyme." The muscles in the small intestine then mix your food with more digestive juices from the pancreas, liver, and intestine and push the mixture forward for further digestion.

The small intestines absorb water and the digested nutrients into your bloodstream. The contents that are not absorbed become waste products and will move into the large intestine. The large intestines then take the waste products from the digestive process, undigested parts of food, fluid, and old cells shed from the lining of your GI tract. The large intestine absorbs water, changing the waste from liquid to formed feces. Once in the bowel, further peristalsis helps the feces to release from your rectum out through the anus.

Special Organs that Help Us Get the Most Out of Our Food

Stomach

Glands in your stomach make stomach acid and enzymes that break down your food. The muscles in your stomach then mix the food with these digestive juices. The stomach will have difficulty digesting your food and retrieving its nutrients if it is more alkaline than it should be. Stomach acid should stay between a pH of 1.5-3.5. High stomach acid is also used to fend off harmful bacteria. An alkaline diet often results in malabsorption; over time, followers of alkaline diets become low in essential nutrients like calcium, iron, zinc, and B12.

Note: The hormone Ghrelin is made by specialized cells in your stomach and pancreas, which we will cover later in this chapter.

Pancreas

The pancreas creates pancreatic juices called enzymes. These enzymes break down the sugar, fat, and starches we eat. The pancreas aids your digestive system by producing hormones. These hormones are insulin, proinsulin, amylin-C peptide, somatostatin, polypeptide, and glucagon. Insulin is the hormone we are most familiar with. Insulin will lower blood sugar, while glucagon will increase blood sugar. The main job of the pancreas is to keep these two hormones in balance. When the pancreas is not functioning properly, problems arise, such as type 1 diabetes, type 2 diabetes, pre-diabetes, and insulin resistance. Below is a quick summary of how each disease stems from a dysregulated pancreas.

<u>Type 1 Diabetes (TD1-Diabetes Mellitus):</u>

Type 1 diabetes is a chronic autoimmune condition that

is not lifestyle-related and not reversible. This occurs when the pancreas makes little or no insulin. The body requires insulin to move sugar (glucose) into the cells to produce energy. Because the sugar is not moving into the cells, blood glucose levels become too high. 90% of people with type 1 diabetes are born with it (it is genetic)and will require insulin injections for life. There is a growing amount of evidence that suggests a ketogenic diet can assist with lowering A1C levels.

The symptoms of type 1 diabetes are as follows:

- Unusual thirst
- Frequent urination
- Poor bladder control
- Bedwetting in children
- Increased hunger
- Weight loss
- Irritability and mood swings
- Feelings of exhaustion
- Blurred vision

Without medication, patients may experience diabetic shock, seizures, and possible coma.

Type 2 Diabetes:

Type 2 diabetes occurs when the body becomes dysfunctional in using glucose. This dysregulated process causes high glucose levels in the blood, leading to other problems in how your body stores fat. At this point, your liver and pancreas are so over-taxed that the body can no longer take up the glucose from your blood. People with type 2 diabetes often end up with NAFLD (non-alcoholic fatty liver disease) or NASH (non-alcoholic steatohepatitis). This occurs when the islet cells in the pancreas release hormones in response to the blood sugar levels, causing the liver to either increase or decrease glucose production. This process will lead to scarring of the liver.

Type 2 diabetes can be reversible as it is caused primarily by diet (the overconsumption of carbs, starches, and sugars) and lifestyle (inactivity). Insulin resistance is the precursor to type 2 diabetes.

Symptoms of type 2 diabetes include:

- Increased thirst/hunger
- Fatigue
- Frequent urination
- Weight loss
- Blurred vision
- Frequent infections
- slow wound healing

The doctor will order blood/lab tests, and they will perform two tests:

1. Fasting glucose. If the levels are 126 mg/dL (7 mmol/L) or higher, then you have type 2 diabetes.

2. The second test is A1C, and if that is over 140 mg/dl (6.5 mmol/L), you are in the type 2 diabetic range.

At this point, your doctor will suggest a drug (usually Metformin or Ozempic – a semaglutide) to treat type 2 diabetes. Many other drugs are currently available in the market. However, by treating type 2 diabetes with a strict ketogenic diet, an exercise regime, and proper sleep habits, you may be able to avoid any pharmaceuticals. I recommend you try this approach first for three months and then request to have your blood sugar levels retested.

Insulin Resistance:

Insulin resistance is when the cells in your muscles, fat, and liver fail to respond to insulin. The body then has a difficult time taking up glucose from your blood. Your pancreas then produces more insulin to help glucose enter your cells. This leaves you with a high blood sugar level (increased A1C and fasting glucose level). The key signs of insulin resistance are a waistline over 40 inches in men (over 35 inches in women), skin tags, and high blood pressure (130/80 or higher). The symptoms you may notice are as follows:

- Extreme thirst or hunger
- Frequent urination
- Tingling in hands or feet
- Fatigue

- Frequent infections
- High blood sugar levels

Insulin resistance may be treated with a low-carb or ketogenic diet and a solid exercise program that includes resistance training.

Pre-Diabetes:

Pre-diabetes is when you have a higher-than-normal blood sugar level on a blood test (A1C of 6.0-6.4). At this point, it's not high enough to be considered type 2 diabetes, but it is on the trajectory. Without lifestyle changes, adults and children with pre-diabetes are at high risk of developing type 2 diabetes. I recommend that adults follow a low-carb or ketogenic diet and an exercise program for three months, then retest their blood sugar levels. For children, I suggest that they start on the Mediterranean diet (very clean eating, whole foods, no sugar or processed foods) and an exercise plan. Perhaps consider signing them up for a sport they are interested in. Have them retest again after three months to see if the blood sugar levels are lowering.

Liver

The liver is a critical organ and is responsible for over 500 functions. The most essential functions are the filtration of toxins, digestion, the emulsification of fats, metabolism, detoxification, protein synthesis, and storing vitamins and minerals. It's in the liver that vitamin D is created by converting it to 25OHD. The skin, kidneys, and our beautiful sunshine assist with the process. Vitamin D deficiency is directly linked to liver disease like cirrhosis. Increasing your vitamin D levels may help to heal your liver.

Our liver can only handle approximately 24 g of natural sugar daily (6 tsp). This should be natural sugar from fruits, vegetables, and grains. Any added sugar during the day (like a donut or candy) will put extra stress on the liver and raise your blood sugar. Sugar is just as toxic to the liver as alcohol.

When it comes to alcohol, the liver can only handle approximately one to two drinks a day: one drink a day for women and two drinks a day for men (4 oz). When you drink alcohol, your liver will stop its other functions (like fat burning) to process that poison to rid the body of it quickly.

Fructose (from fresh fruits, fruit juices, dried fruits, and ultra-processed foods) dramatically affects the liver because it has difficulty metabolizing a quantity. Overconsumption of fructose taxes the liver, thus causing NAFLD (non-alcoholic fatty liver disease) and NASH (Non-alcoholic steatohepatitis). On a positive note, the liver is the only organ in the body that can regenerate itself.

I never recommend liver "cleanses" as they are harsh on the liver, can stress other organs, and push the toxins from the liver into the rest of the body. These cleanses often leave you feeling worse than before. Instead, I tell patients to eat very clean for a month or two if they have been eating a lot of sugar or ultra-processed foods.

If you want to clean your liver, here is what I suggest: drink water with lemon wedges, avoid alcohol, avoid all ultra-processed foods, avoid deep-fried food, avoid sugar, avoid pop, avoid energy drinks, avoid excess fruits (try one whole fruit a day). You should eat whole-natural foods, which is everything we have discussed so far. Prepare and cook your food. Stay focused on green vegetables, good quality meats, eggs and fats, dairy, nuts and seeds, and one fruit daily (preferably dark berries). Avoid rice and grains for four to eight weeks. Drink lots of water and herbal tea.

While you are doing this whole food liver cleanse, I always prescribe the supplement milk thistle (silybum marianum). Several scientific studies have shown that phytochemicals in milk thistle (the flavonoid called silymarin) protect the liver from toxins.

Note: The contraindication for milk thistle is that it should not be taken with the following drugs:

- Allergy medication
- Cholesterol-lowering medications
- Anti-anxiety medications
- Blood thinners
- Cancer drugs

These interactions occur because milk thistles may interfere with the efficacy of these drugs as they are all broken down by the same liver enzymes. Women who are pregnant or nursing should not take milk thistle, nor should anyone with a history of hormone-related cancers. Also, those with allergies to ragweed or chamomile should avoid milk thistle.

If you are not dealing with contraindications, I recommend taking milk thistle as a supplement with your clean-eating liver cleanse. I suggest taking about 150 mg of milk thistle three times a day with food. If you want to take milk thistle, do so for only six months, then stop.

The Three Main Hormones We Need to Pay Attention to

The hormones I speak the most about are Insulin, Ghrelin, and Leptin. We have already talked about insulin, and most of us are familiar with this hormone, but many people have not heard about the "hormone" friends: Ghrelin and Leptin. Let's look at these two hormones and how they are affected by the foods we eat.

Ghrelin:

Ghrelin is a hormone produced mainly in the cells of the stomach (P/D1 cells) and pancreas (epsilon cells). Ghrelin is the hormone that makes you feel hungry. I always tell patients to think of Ghrelin as the Gremlin living in the stomach; it always wants food. The more you feed Ghrelin, the more it wants to eat. The foods that trigger the activation of the Ghrelin hormone are:

- Simple carbohydrates
- Sugar
- Starchy vegetables
- Fruits high on the glycemic index
- Ultra-processed foods
- Sugary drinks
- Junk foods

When you eat these foods, your blood sugar spikes and then falls. The Ghrelin wants more of the same food as soon as the blood sugar falls again. Have you ever noticed that you could eat an entire bag of cookies or a family-size bag of chips, yet a couple of hours later, you feel hungry again? This is the effect of the Ghrelin hormone. By avoiding these foods, you can control that hormone. Many people take the L-cysteine supplement to control their hunger, but you can do this through whole foods. L-cysteine (an amino acid) can be obtained from animal products like eggs, beef, chicken, fish, and full-fat dairy.

Leptin:

Leptin is a hormone found in your adipose tissue and the small intestine. Leptin suppresses hunger, makes you feel full, and regulates your energy. This hormone helps you to maintain a healthy weight and assists you in weight loss. Think of it this way: Ghrelin makes you hungry, but Leptin leaps in to save you! Leptin was my superhero during my weight loss journey. The more Leptin-type foods I consumed, the thinner I became.

The Leptin hormone can be turned on by:

- Heme protein and fats (meat, fish, poultry)
- Full-fat dairy products (butter, ghee, cheese, yogurt, sour cream, full-fat cream)
- Good fats (coconut oil, MCT oil, olive oil, avocado oils)
- Nuts and seeds

Low glycemic fruits and greens slide under the radar on this hormone; they don't seem to spike Ghrelin. Another component of increasing Leptin is not overeating or eating between meals. If you are eating Leptin-friendly foods, aim for two to three meals a day and try to avoid snacking in between. You can do this by eating enough of the right foods at your main meals. Another good practice is to stop eating three hours before sleep.

Note: *New research into the Leptin hormone has shown that in obese patients, adding an Omega 3 supplement to their diet increased Leptin. However, those with a proper BMI weight did not show a drastic rise in Leptin when taking an Omega 3 supplement.*

Our bodies are wonderfully created, and the food we put into them matters. Every cell, organ, and hormone plays a role in processing food, and we don't often think about that. Whenever I take a new client or speak at an engagement, I talk about the organs and hormones and how they process food. Once you understand your body, you have the keys to take control of your health. When our mind is opened to the fact that we only have one body for this life, we can choose to take care of it or abuse it. Hence, the truth is that what we feed our bodies now will affect our health later in life. If we take care of our organs and hormones, we will reap the health benefits for life.

Summary of Chapter 11

A calorie is not just a calorie. What we eat affects our organs and hormones and can make us put on unnecessary pounds. Those excess pounds can create inflammation and blood sugar dysregulation, leading to many health complications. Eat foods your liver, pancreas, and hormones will love!

1. In the first part of this chapter, we recapped the digestive system and how we process food.
2. We spoke about the stomach and how it plays a vital function in breaking down food by churning it using high-acid stomach juices. We also spoke about how important it is for our stomach acid to

have a high pH level so that it not only breaks down food but also kills bacteria.

3. The pancreas is another vital organ for breaking down food and balancing blood sugar levels. We covered the hormones produced in the liver and how the pancreas balances insulin and glucagon. We also looked at the issues that arise from a dysregulated pancreas (type 1 diabetes, type 2 diabetes, insulin resistance, and pre-diabetes).

4. We covered the liver and its vitality. The liver performs over 500 functions. Sugar, fructose, and alcohol are difficult for the liver to process. The liver can only handle approximately 24 g (6 tsp) of natural sugar and one to two drinks of alcohol per day. The liver is the only organ that can completely regenerate.

5. We discussed the hormone Ghrelin, which is produced in the stomach and pancreas. Ghrelin is triggered by simple carbs, sugar, fructose, and starches, and increases appetite.

6. Leptin is another hormone that holds the key to weight loss. Leptin is found in the adipose tissue and small intestines. It is triggered by animal protein, dairy, and good fats. When these foods are consumed, Leptin decreases your appetite.

Takeaway from Chapter 11:

Organs and hormones are crucial in regulating our appetite and absorbing nutrients.

How Food Affects Hormones and Organs

Chapter 12
The Canada Food Guide and the Standard America Diet

Why are our government-recommended diets not the healthiest option?

We are well aware that food is big business in North America. There are so many choices, voices, and opinions about food that it can make your head spin. If you read one research paper about food, there are three contradictory arguments. Most people don't read through those papers to see who funded or authored the research; they often just read a research title and accept it as fact without reading it through.

The following is an example: an article was published in the International Journal of Obesity (November 2015), which apparently proved that diet drinks were better than water for weight loss. To any nutritionist, that would seem nonsensical. However, if you read through to the end, you will find that Coca-Cola and PepsiCo were members of that piece of research. Not only that, but the group directly paid the researchers to conduct the study. This is a direct conflict of interest, which is only one example of a rigged study.

On top of all the choices, we have to deal with false statements printed on our food labels. Canada is one of the worst countries for food labeling. Europe has a far more advanced system for label transparency. This is not so in North America, where there are fewer food-label restrictions. Ultra-processed foods, even products that aren't "real food," have Canadian labels on them touting "Healthy," "Nutritious," "Heart Healthy," "Sugar-free," "Fat-free" and without fail, these products are usually not what they claim to be. Most contain nothing but sugar or aspartame, high fructose corn syrup, poor-quality oils, chemicals, and additives.

Food companies spend billions every year to market to various ages (especially kids), races, sexes, and even provinces or states. Your food should not have to be labeled as "nutritious," and it should not be marketed to you. Have you ever noticed that there is no label on apples, lettuce, or steak? Real food doesn't require labels. I've never seen a commercial begging us to eat asparagus.

As a society, we should instinctively know what real food is and that it is good for us. However, we are the only species that seems confused about what to eat. Instead, we rely on food companies and government food agencies to tell us what we should consume. Giving an agency or person control over your eating is a slippery slope. It gives them the "power" over your health.

The more we follow the guidance of government nutritional agencies, the sicker we seem to become as a society. The end result is the only people profiting are the major food corporations, industrial farmers, and pharmaceutical companies. This insanity has to stop at some point; we need to come to a place where we buy real food, prepare real food, and eat real food.

The powers that exist want to make food complicated. Now, hear me when I say their aim is to confuse you so you give up reading your labels and trying to eat healthy. They will win if they fill our minds with conflicting research that causes confusion within us. Once we are confused, various agencies can come in like saviors and tell us how to eat and what foods to purchase. The truth, however, is that it is not complicated at all. What have we eaten for thousands of years? Real food and only real food is what your body requires.

In a perfect world, our healthcare system would encourage patients to see a nutritionist as a front-line health support before prescribing pharmaceuticals. Patients can often change various health issues by eating a whole foods diet, adding exercise or movement, learning to deal with stress properly, and learning sleep protocol to get appropriate sleep.

When I brought this suggestion to doctors, the response was usually, “Patient compliance is low; most people won't follow a proper diet or stay committed to an exercise regime, so it is pointless.” However, I disagree. I have more faith in patients. I myself was one of those overweight and sick patients. If people are given the tools to succeed, many will follow through. We should at least give them a chance to take control of their own health.

Now, let’s take a look at North American food guides, such as the Canadian Food Guide and the Standard American Diet. What are they telling us as a society to eat? To do that properly, we must walk through history to see how both came to be.

The Canada Food Guide

Canada's Food Guide began with the unethical experimentation involving our First Nations people and residential schools. Fifty years after the introduction of the Indian Act (1876), First Nation peoples living on reserves were malnourished due to a lack of adequate and safe food supplies. Rather than going onto the reserves and assisting them with food or food programs, scientists and government officials decided to use the opportunity to conduct nutritional experiments on them. An article was published in 2013 by author Ian Mosby titled “Administering Colonial Science: Nutrition Research and Human Biomedical Experimentation in Aboriginal Communities and Residential Schools" (1942-1952). Mosby would expose some of the atrocities during this period in Canadian history.

In the article, Mosby speaks about the severe and unethical experiments performed on nearly 1000 children within six different residential schools throughout Canada. In these schools, the First Nation children were fed barely enough to keep them alive, often only being given 30% of the daily calories they required. They referred to this as the baseline.

Although the schools did receive government funding to support the children's nutritional needs, meats, cheese, eggs, fresh fruits, fresh vegetables, and salt were rarely available. They mainly lived off of cornflakes, scraps, oats, fortified flour, and rotted fruit and vegetables. Residential school-based nutrition experiments and examinations were part of a more extensive investigation into the diets of First Nation children.

These nutritional experiments would keep track of the baseline of malnutrition (basically, how little food could be given to keep them alive). They would then test both nutrition intervention and non-interventional approaches.

Biochemist Lionell Pett led these studies. Pett had a theory that the "Indian problem" was caused by malnutrition. Pett oversaw the experiments conducted in residential schools and was, and still is, considered the father of Canadian nutrition.

One of Petts's experiments included testing the effects of the consumption of fortified flour on children. At that time, fortified flour was banned in Canada. The outcome of the fortified flour experiment did not end well. There was a massive rise in anemia in these children. They were being used as human guinea pigs. Science wanted to know the minimum nutritional requirements necessary to keep people alive, not necessarily thrive.

Other experiments conducted by Pett would later expand into examining the effects of various vitamins and minerals on children's health. Once again, using the baseline of malnutrition, researchers would provide nutrition interventions using both controlled and intervention groups. This allowed researchers to provide vitamin/mineral supplementation to some while other children were given placebos. They would then monitor how sick or how healthy different groups of children would become.

This set of experiments would form the basis for "Canada's Food Rules," later termed the Canadian Food Guide. The unethical experiments and the abusive treatment these researchers carried out would forever alter the health of these children and their own families.

The purpose of the Canada Food Guide today is to let citizens know what the government agency, Health Canada (the Office of Nutrition Policy and Promotion/and the Canadian Council on Nutrition), believes we should eat. These agencies consult with external advisory boards to gather suggestions on what should be added to the food guide or removed from it. The various professionals that sit on that board work together to create the food guide based on the most current "research."

People carry their own biases, and we know that research papers can be skewed in one way or another. Here are some fictitious scenarios that could occur on these advisory boards: what if several vegetarians on the board bring research that only favors vegetarianism? Another situation might arise if a board member holds stocks in a grain or soybean company trading on the TSE. Perhaps a board member's brother owns a specific food company that may profit from certain changes in the food guide.

As I said, these scenarios are fictitious, but you can see how conflicts of interest could appear on any advisory board. In addition to the situation, specific food lobbyists are pushing for their products to be added to the food guide while other food lobbyists petition to remove certain groups from the food guide so that they can promote their products.

Once the Canada Food Guide is compiled, it directly influences what doctors, nurses, and dietitians tell patients about food choices. They are obliged to comply with the Canada Food Guide. These food recommendations are then taught in every school, college, and university as the nutritional gold standard. It leaves no room for individual eating plans. As a side note, a relatively new doctor I spoke with told me he was surprised that he was only offered 25 hours of nutritional training over his years of studying medicine. He added that the information appeared to be outdated, yet doctors and nurses continue giving out nutritional advice instead of referring patients to nutritional professionals.

They dictate a one-size-fits-all approach to people's health; there is never a recommendation outside this box. There seems to be a real avoidance of acknowledging that their food recommendations do not work for everyone. We are not robots coming off an assembly line. We all have different nutritional needs from one another. That is why this one-size-fits-all dietary recommendation has never worked and will never work.

Our food guide has gone through various changes over the last 74 years. The Canada Food Guide of the 1950s was a far more balanced diet that included all Canadian-grown products. The food guide of the 50s and much of the 60s contained dairy (¼ plate), animal protein (¼ plate), fruits and vegetables combined (¼ plate), bread, and cereal (¼ plate). This older food guide (shown below) represents all Canadian food growers, including meat, poultry, grain, fruit and vegetable growers, and dairy farmers. These are the foods our ancestors thrived on for centuries.

The Early Canada Food Guide (Dairy, Meat, Grains, Fruit, and Vegetables)

Over the years, our governing agencies have continued to increase the amount of grains, legumes, fruits, and vegetables we are expected to consume. At the same time, they began decreasing the amount of dairy, meat, and fats. As a nutritionist, I am thrilled to see more fresh vegetables and the commitment to whole fruits (instead of juicing), but I have a real problem with so many grains and legumes, as most people cannot properly digest them.

I also would never recommend diabetics, those who are insulin resistant, or those with metabolic syndrome or NAFLD to consume grains and legumes. We also have to consider those who have Celiac disease, non-Celiac disease, gluten and wheat allergies, or gluten sensitivities. What are they to eat now that Canada is trying to lower our diet's meat, dairy, and fat? There are gluten-free bread and other products; however, they are highly processed and contain preservatives, emulsifiers, food-grade chemicals, sugar, and/or high fructose corn syrup.

The Canada Food Guide recommendations also impact our health by decreasing the fat we require for our brain health and hormones. In addition, we require animal protein to stave off anemia (B12 deficiency, iron deficiency, zinc deficiency). Tofu and legumes will not build blood the way heme protein does.

Another problem with decreasing meat and dairy (for those who can consume dairy) is that it is causing real turmoil for our Canadian meat, poultry, and dairy farmers. Many producers are struggling, and some of our family farms are collapsing. This will absolutely have an impact on our Canadian economy.

We spoke in the introduction about the war of the two hypotheses back in the 1950s. John Yudkins' hypothesis (Britain) claimed sugar was destroying our health, while Ancel Keys' hypothesis (America) claimed it was saturated fat. Due to Keys' power and influence, his hypothesis won out, and America, then Canada, began following a low fat (lower animal protein) high carb/sugar diet. Remember, excess fruit (fructose) and all grains convert to sugar in the liver and spike both insulin and the hormone Ghrelin. We can see the result of that low-fat, high-carb diet in our society today. People are fatter and sicker, and our healthcare system is becoming over-taxed. A 2021 statistic from Statcan.gc.ca reveals that 67% (two-thirds) of Canadians take a medication. That's stunning!

By the early 2000s, we saw the Canadian Food Guide move towards a more plant-based diet. This is a very deficient diet for most in our population. Think about our First Nations people who live off of hunting and fishing. Meat and fat are staples in their culture. It's obvious that cultural eating methods were not considered in this food guide.

Now cut to January 22, 2019, and here we see the brand-new Canada Food Guide, which focuses on a plant-based diet. They finally did it; the majority of the food was grains, legumes, vegetables, fruit, tofu, a few bites of animal protein, and the removal of fat and dairy. What could possibly go wrong?

The plate above focuses on plant protein, lots of grains, legumes, fruit, and vegetables, only a mouthful of animal protein, and removing fat and dairy. Health Canada is now promoting a "plant/grain-based diet" to Canadians for optimal health.

The five main problems with the new Canada Food Guide are:

- Most people have a difficult time digesting wheat, gluten, and legumes. Where does that leave all those who have to avoid grains and legumes, like those with Celiac disease, non-Celiac disease, gluten/wheat allergies, insulin resistance, metabolic syndrome, diabetes, and those who are already very anemic? We are sacrificing the majority for a few who loudly push us toward a plant-based diet at all costs.

- This is culturally insulting to those of us (including our First Nations people) who thrive on hunting and fishing not only for food but for cultural reasons as well.

- The Canadian meat and poultry farmers contribute a lot to the Canadian economy. The Canadian beef sector alone contributes over $24 billion to Canada's GDP annually, while dairy farmers contribute over $15 billion annually. When our Canadian farmers start going out of business, will we increase the multi-cropped GMO'd soybeans, corn, and grains to make that money back?

- With this new food guide, there is no focus on good fats to feed hormones (increasing leptin) and preserving brain health. Saturated fat continues to be vilified even after unveiling new research to the contrary. The focus remains on a high-carbohydrate diet. There is no mention of olive oil, coconut oil, avocado oil, grass-fed butter, or ghee being added to food to help with absorption.

- The Canadian Food Guide takes a one-size-fits-all approach, and we are individual humans who must adapt to a way of eating that is right for each person. Government-approved dieticians (as well as doctors and nurses) are expected to promote the Canadian Food Guide as a type of "food bible," so this will always be the recommended diet of choice for each and every patient. On the contrary, holistic nutritionists can recommend a variety of dietary changes suited to each patient's individual needs.

The good part of the Canadian Food Guide is that it recommends whole fresh foods and avoids junk food and ultra-processed food. It has also added the importance of water, which is a positive addition.

Does the Standard American Diet fare any better?

The Standard American Diet (SAD) is based on a consensus of mainstream government-licensed “nutritional experts.” It is compiled from data gathered from the National Health and Nutrition Examination Survey and recommendations from food lobbyists.

The original (RDA) "Recommended Dietary Allowance" came into existence during World War II when Lydia J. Roberts, Hazel Stiebeling, and Helen S. Mitchell introduced it. They sat on a committee established by the United States National Academy of Sciences to examine how nutrition might affect national defense.

During World War II (1943), the first edition of the Recommended Dietary Allowances (RDA) was released to the public. The RDA set out to create a standard of proper nutrition for all Americans. It would lay out the daily allowances of specific foods and nutrient values for people of various ages. Between 1943 and 1950, the RDA largely reflected the food groups that most Americans were already eating.

Below, we see “A Guide to Good Eating” (1950).

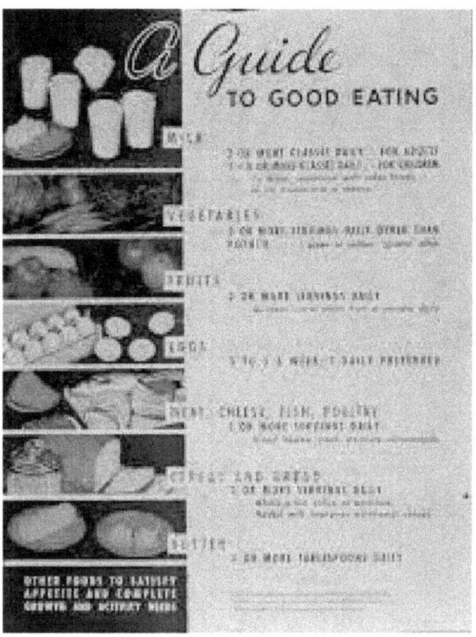

Here, we can still see a wide variety of foods our great-grandparents would have consumed. It suggested real food such as dairy, vegetables, fruit, meat, grains, and butter. These foods would have been on the plate of every farming family.

Compare that to the 2020 Standard American Diet. It’s not as bad as Canada’s Food Guide, but it’s getting close. Grains are now the foundation of the American food pyramid. Fruits and vegetables, low amounts of dairy and meat, and a sparing amount of fat. In another five years, they will be on par with Canada, heading to a plant-based, high-carb diet.

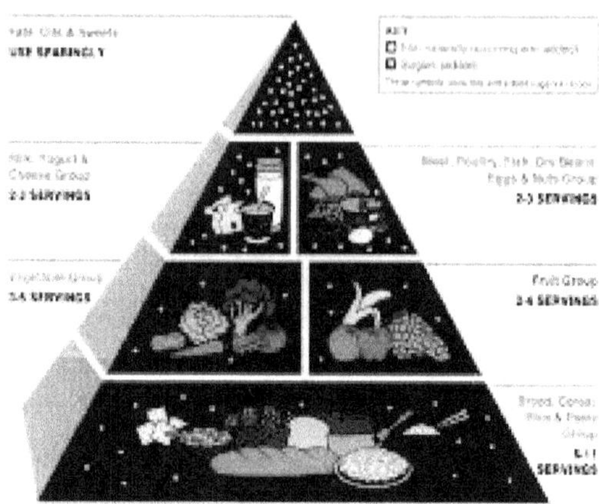

So, once again, we see the influence of Ancel Keys' hypothesis: fat is villainized, and carbohydrates/sugar is healthy. Since the late 1960s, the American diet has been pushed towards this high-carb, low-fat way of eating. I urge you to look around at Americans today and see the results for yourself.

Currently, in the USA, 32.6 million Americans have type 2 diabetes, and 88 million people suffer from prediabetes (36.7% of the population). Many healthcare professionals link this to the following of the Standard American Diet (government food pyramid). The problem continues to be that carbohydrates are broken down into sugar within the liver. The carbohydrates not burned off by activity are stored as fat. Consuming fat does not spike insulin. So when SAD lowers the fat and protein intake (which raises Leptin and lowers blood sugar) and increases the carbohydrates, fruits, and starchy vegetables (which raises Ghrelin and blood sugar), they end up with issues such as obesity, insulin resistance, and metabolic syndrome.

According to Statista, the USA was the number one country that consumed the most pharmaceuticals in 2022. Germany came in second and Canada third. This is not something any of us should be proud of. If the nutritional advice we are being given is so sound, why are both of our countries on so many medications? France has a far lower rate of pharmaceutical use per capita.

Have you ever been to France? If you have, you would have noticed that most of the population is thin to average in size. You don't see obesity in French culture like in North America. In France, people still eat animal fat, animal protein, and a lot of dairy. They use butter (not margarine), deep fry with lard or tallow (not vegetable or seed oils), and one of their favorite dishes is fondu (meat or bread dipped in cheese).

The average French person eats a total of 108 grams of saturated fat daily, while Americans consume roughly 72 grams of fat per day. The SAD recommends staying under 50 grams of fat daily and increasing carbohydrates to 325 grams. In Canada, the CFG recommends that Canadians consume 30 grams of saturated fat daily and 300 grams of carbs daily. North America is eating completely differently from our French brothers and sisters. If America and Canada flip our food pyramids upside down, we would eat like the French.

The French also eat smaller portions and are not always hungry. Consuming saturated fats and animal protein keeps you satiated longer, and you are not ravenous. This is due to the fat, dairy, and protein-raising Leptin (the hunger suppression hormone). The French eat grains (which are not as processed as ours), and the desserts are served in much smaller portions.

North Americans eat three times the amount of food the French eat in one sitting. Then, they unbuckle their pants to make room for dessert. That Ghrelin hormone triggered by the sugar, carbs, and excess fructose is like a Gremlin that they have to keep feeding. Food and how our hormones respond to it create this crazy loop that keeps us wanting more.

I personally believe that is why food companies are marketing ultra-processed foods containing sugar, refined grains, high fructose corn syrup, trans fat, and additives that make us addicted. They want us to buy more and eat more to increase that Ghrelin hormone and stay hungry. When we eat more of their products, the food companies make money. Remember Lays potato chips slogan, "Betcha can't eat just one!"

Have you ever noticed that food companies are not pushing us to consume chicken breasts, vegetables, butter, or cheese? Think about this: if a country were to take fat, dairy, and animal protein off the food guide, it would make the citizens insatiably hungry while becoming addicted to the very foods they were eating. Eventually, they would become overweight and unhealthy and lose control of their health. But I guess that's what pharmaceutical companies are there for.

Summary of Chapter 12

We looked at the Canadian Food Guide and the Standard American Diet recommendations. Both have changed radically over the years, moving from a diet our ancestors ate for centuries to more of a plant/grain-based diet. We also discussed the problems both have caused as they try to decrease animal fat, protein, and dairy and promote a diet heavy on grains, legumes, vegetables, and fruit.

The other point we covered is that these food guides don't consider those who sustain themselves through hunting and fishing. This involves our First Nations people, who have lived off animal fat and protein for thousands of years. It was the introduction of processed grains, GMO corn, sugar, and alcohol that caused the issues they currently have with their health.

We also took a look at how the French eat and why their country has the lowest rate of obesity while consuming a much higher amount of animal fat, animal protein, and dairy.

Takeaway from Chapter 12:

I don't recommend either of our country's food guides. I am with the French on this one, and not just because I am part French! I very firmly believe we should be eating real whole foods: lots of fresh vegetables, 1-3 in-season fresh fruit a day, a decent amount of good fats, full-fat dairy (if you can digest it), and daily servings of meat, poultry and lots of fish. Everyone will have a way of eating that is right for their body, but eating natural, whole, fresh foods is a great foundation to build on. I don't think any government should dictate what their citizens put into their mouths.

The Canada Food Guide and the Standard America Diet

Chapter 13
The 4 Keys to Health: Food, Exercise, Stress Management, and Sleep

We have talked a lot about the first key to health, "food." By now, you are aware that I am a big proponent of fresh, local fruit and vegetables, as well as locally sourced meat and dairy. We also covered some basic biology so you understand how your body processes food and how that food affects your organs and hormones.

After that short recap, we must discuss three other important keys to your health and longevity. These keys would be exercise, the reduction of stress, and proper sleep. As previously discussed, our bodies are complex and wonderfully designed. Many variants can affect our health. If your nutrition is on par, but you are stressed and not sleeping, your body will suffer. If all the other components are in place but you are inactive, your body will also suffer. These four must be in balance.

Let's look at the importance of each key and how we can make changes to create a well-rounded health program. Our ultimate goal should always be two-fold: optimum health and longevity.

Exercise: The Importance of Exercise and Body Movement

As a personal trainer and a self-proclaimed "exercise nut," this is my second favorite topic after food! When I talk about exercise and movement, I break it down into four parts to create one fully functional program.

- Cardio
- Weight resistance
- Balance
- Stretching

We require all four components to create a healthy exercise regime. You really can't separate them. If you are only focusing on cardio and avoid strength training, your body will become unbalanced. If you are only weightlifting, you will neglect your cardiovascular system. When you omit balancing practices, you will lose coordination in your senior years. Failure to stretch will open you up to various injuries.

Let's break down what each component does, why it is needed, and how to put it into practice.

Cardio

What do we define as cardio? Cardio is any exercise that works out the heart. While the heart is pumping, our bodies grow more blood vessels by expanding our web of capillaries. So, cardio works out our heart and can lower our blood pressure and strengthen our blood vessels. Cardio acts as a vasodilator, increasing the blood flow to both the body and the brain. In the brain, that blood flow increases the size of the hippocampus, which leads to improved memory and the ability to learn new things. Cardio also works for those of us with ADHD by calming and helping our minds to focus.

Allow me to give you an example. When I was in college (as an adult), I would have a lot of anxiety before exams—having ADHD made exam times brutal because any distraction would make me lose my focus and stop my ability to recall information. I was already a long-distance runner at that time, and one of my professors suggested that I take a 30-minute run before my exam to see if that would help. I was skeptical, but I complied. Forty-five minutes before my biochem exam, I took off for a run around the waterfront. I came back to the exam room and was amazed at how all the information was organized in my brain, and I was hyper-focused. I did amazingly well on that exam, and from that time on, I ran to reset my ability to focus and recall information. I still use exercise today to lower my ADHD symptoms.

Almost every personal training client I've had has asked, "What is the best form of cardio?” I always answer the same way, "Whatever you love to do that raises your heart rate." Why try a form of cardio you dislike? If you love to walk, power walk. If you love to swim, do laps. Perhaps bike riding is your niche. It doesn't matter what cardio you do; as long as you enjoy it, you will stick to it. I suggest 30 minutes of cardio 4-5 times a week. You aim to get your heart rate up and sustain it for at least 15-20 minutes. Begin slowly when warming up; once you begin breathing heavier, stay in that zone for 15-20 minutes, then slow down at the end to cool your body down.

We have all heard about maximum heart rate, but how do we figure that out? The way to calculate your maximum heart rate is to subtract your age from 220, which gives you your maximum heart rate. Remember that this is your peak level and only a guide. You know your heart rate is increasing if you are breathy and can talk periodically but not sing.

How do you fit cardio into your day? You can do this in several ways:

- Walk or bike to work.
- Join a gym and use the cardio equipment before or after work.
- Use your lunch break for a power walk or climbing stairs.
- Wake up early and follow a YouTube cardio program.
- Walk your dog at a slightly faster pace on your daily walks.

What are the other benefits of cardio? Cardio burns excess carbohydrates first, and once the carbs are burned off, you begin to burn fat. To get to the fat-burning stage, you will need to extend your cardio time and intensity. Cardio will continue to burn for a short time after you complete your session, but it doesn't continue burning at rest.

Weight Resistance

The term "weight resistance" refers to strength training or weight lifting. Weight resistance is used to build muscle strength and anaerobic endurance and to increase bone density. No exercise program is complete without weight resistance.

Why is weightlifting necessary? When it comes to weight loss or maintaining a healthy weight, resistance training is very important. When you build muscle, it strengthens your musculoskeletal system, helps protect your joints from injury, burns more fat, and makes you look fabulous. Muscle burns fat, so the more muscle you have, the more your metabolism revs up and the more fat you burn. This accelerates weight loss more so than cardio. Muscle burns fat while you are working out and also while you are at rest. It is a 24-hour burning system, and it gives your body great definition! Weightlifting can be done well into your elderly years.

To prove this point, let me introduce you to my hero! A female weight lifter named Ernestine Shepherd from Baltimore, Maryland, USA. She has been labeled the "6-pack Granny" and has the title of the oldest female bodybuilder, according to Guinness World Records (2010-2011). At 86 years old, she competed regularly and looked amazing. There was no rocking chair or knitting in her future! I intend to follow her example!

How do you weight train, and how often? You should aim for 3-4 times a week with a one-day rest in between to give your muscles time to repair. Some people choose to do a full-body workout (each muscle group); others prefer to split their sessions into various days, focusing on legs, back and chest, arms, and abdominals. To do this, you will need to hit the gym more frequently. To see results, you have to work out each muscle group at least three times a week.

This is where I am going to give a huge plug for personal training. There are a lot of techniques for lifting weights. You need to have some guidance from a personal trainer to begin a weight resistance program. You need to have them check your form, determine how heavy the weights should be, how to increase weight, how to use the equipment properly, and how to stretch after. Most gyms offer at least one personal training session, so make use of it. I have personally seen too many people lifting improperly or using equipment wrong and incurring injuries. A trainer will give you a program to follow, ensure your form is good, and explain how to execute each exercise so that you see improvements.

Balance

What is balance training? Balance training involves performing exercises that strengthen the muscles that keep your body aligned; these include both legs and your abdominals (core). These exercises are designed to improve stability and coordination and increase your reaction time. Continually working on balance will help prevent falls, not only now but as you age. Balance exercises can be added to the end of your workout session just before stretching. Yoga or pilates classes are wonderful ways to work on both balance and stretching.

Note: Balance begins to decline after the age of 40 and rapidly declines by the age of 65. However, we can counteract that decline by working balance training in our weekly workouts. Ask your trainer to incorporate balance training into your program or take some classes.

Stretching

We need to stretch, especially after our workouts, to keep the muscles flexible and healthy. Stretching increases our flexibility and helps us maintain our range of motion within our joints. When we don't stretch properly, the muscles shorten and then tighten. If you don't stretch often and or properly, the muscles tighten to the point that they won't fully extend. This can lead to many injuries, such as iliotibial band issues or very tight hamstrings. Injuries caused by overuse and not stretching properly may take you right out of the game.

Don't stretch before working out; that is no longer recommended. Cardio or a good walk is enough to warm your muscles before exercise. Never do bouncing stretches; these can cause injuries, especially if your muscles are not warmed up. I recommend all my clients perform static stretches (stretch and hold still) at the very end of their workout. Stretch each muscle group for 30-45 seconds each. This gives the muscles time to elongate properly after being shortened during your workout.

Putting it all together

Many people may feel confused as to how to put these four exercise components together, but it is doable. Let's break it down into parts.

1. **Where:** First of all, decide whether you are going to join a gym or set up an exercise program at home.

2. **When:** Once you've made that decision, figure out when your best time to work out would be. For example, I am a 4:30-5:00 am riser, and I like to work out before work.

My husband, on the other hand, loves to work out after work, even as late as 10:00 pm. Time does not matter as much as commitment and consistency.

3. **How:** If you join a gym or a class, then the how is figured out for you. You will have a personal trainer at the gym make you a program or follow an instructor leading a class. If you are doing neither, figure out when you will be walking, riding a bike to work, or swimming at lunch. Then, invest in some home weights and equipment for your weight resistance. The balance and stretching can be done at home following a YouTube video.

4. **Why:** Ask yourself why? What do you want to get out of your exercise regime? Your "WHY" will keep you motivated. Years ago, I was motivated to start exercising again to lose 85 pounds. While raising my kids, I did it for energy, meditation, and to maintain my weight. In college, I exercised for my mental health and to control my ADHD symptoms. Today, I exercise for health, bone density, weight management, and focus. You can see that for every period in my life, I had a specific focus and motivation to stay active. I would not have done it if I didn't have a target or purpose for exercising. So, make a list of your motivations and your "whys." Place that list somewhere you can see it, and let it remind you why it is crucial to get up and start moving.

5. **Flow:** Find a rhythm to make it all flow together. Daily fitness includes some cardio (going for a walk, climbing stairs, riding a bike to work, and trying rollerblading). Three to four times a week, do weight lifting (at a gym, home, or weight resistance class). Three to four times a week, add a few balance exercises (after your weight resistance). Anytime you do cardio or lift weights, remember to perform static stretches with a hold of 30-45 seconds.

We all get busy, and our day can often get away from us; however, our bodies desperately need exercise. Exercise is not only necessary for our body but also for our mind. It will take some dedication and motivation to start. It will become easier once you have your routine down, and you will look forward to your workouts. If you are a person who struggles with self-motivation, I suggest you get together with a partner. This way, you are not alone and can encourage each other. Remember, you deserve to be healthy; see your exercise as an investment in a new you!

Stress: What Does Stress do to Our Body, and How Can We Lower Our Stress?

Have you ever woken up late for work, made the mad dash to the car while still brushing your teeth, then sped off? Just reading that sentence can make you feel the stress in your chest. We have all had those situations, and we can identify with what our bodies and minds go through when we are alarmed, grieved, or shocked. Stress, especially chronic stress, can have devastating long-term consequences on our health.

When we become stressed, the body goes into "fight or flight." This is what our ancestors would experience being chased by a lion. Some might turn and fight the lion, while others would run from the lion. Whichever path they chose, both would experience the same effects of stress. Today, we don't experience the same danger as our ancestors, but our bodies still experience symptoms similar to our current stressors.

Stress releases the hormones adrenaline and cortisol. These hormones cause physical reactions such as elevated heart rate, sweaty hands, increased blood pressure, increased blood sugar levels, and a sudden surge of energy. It is this automatic response that was created in us to react to sudden "acute" stress. *Acute stress* is very different from chronic stress. When our ancestors ran from that lion, once they were safe, they could completely relax; the lion didn't come back every few seconds. Compared to today, our stress is more "*chronic*." Our lions come back not only daily but sometimes minute by minute.

Our current environment is filled with stressors. Due to the high cost of living, we are working harder and longer hours. Most of us are slaves to our cell phones; we consume hours of social media, news clips, tragedies, and wars from around the world. Then we have work deadlines, caring for children, aging parents, accumulative debt, and health issues. People today live in a constant state of stress, and that can put us in a situation where our stress "switch" stays on. We don't have that time to rest after escaping from the lion. There are effects on our body from both acute and chronic stress.

The Effects of Acute Stress

Acute stress (even minor stress) can affect the body by causing stomachaches, headaches, shaking, sweating, and even vomiting. Repeated acute stress, like constantly fighting with a spouse or being in a job you hate, can cause inflammation in the body. This inflammation affects the circulatory system and can contribute to plaque in the coronary arteries. Elevated levels of cortisol will affect your cholesterol levels by raising both your LDL (small particles, not large) and triglyceride levels. The combination of inflammation and raised LDL and triglycerides increases your risk of serious heart disease.

The Effects of Chronic Stress

Chronic stress can have an even more significant impact on your health. When chronic stressors affect your life daily for an extended period, the health impacts can become quite dangerous. This long-term continuation of the release of cortisol, as well as other stress hormones, can wreak havoc on your body and mind. Those effects may be permanent. So, although we often joke about being "stressed out," it is no laughing matter.

Chronic stress increases your risk for a plethora of physical and mental health issues. Chronic stress can appear as:

- Anger and aggression
- Anxiety
- Digestive problems
- Chronic fatigue
- Headaches/migraines
- Depression
- Muscle pain/tension
- Heart disease/heart attacks
- High blood sugar
- High blood pressure
- Insulin resistance
- Metabolic syndrome
- Obesity
- Lowered immune system
- Stroke
- Insomnia/disruptive sleep
- Memory loss
- Concentration impairment
- Increases your risk for dementia/Alzheimer's

We see that stress, both acute and chronic, can be detrimental to our health. What are the steps we can take to lower our stress levels and learn to stay calm? We can do many things, and what works for some may not work for others. Before we get to the steps to control stress, you first have to ask yourself two questions.

1. Is your stress situational?

Is your stress caused by situations such as a toxic relationship, a toxic employment situation, complicated friendships, unemployment, or debt? These are stressors that can be remedied with direct changes. You can take control of these stressors. You will need a sound support system, a good counselor, and perhaps some professional help (ex- debt relief counselor, lawyer, employment counselor, life coach) to help you make some life changes.

2. Is your stress chronic and ongoing?

This may include health conditions, being the primary caregiver for children or spouses with disabilities, or caring for aging parents. These are more difficult to change. With ongoing stress, you will need to find ways to control how the stress affects you and discover ways to reach out for help and take time for yourself. Keep in mind even these stressors won't last forever. Again, build a strong support system, ask for help or delegate when you can, and book time daily for yourself (even if just for 30 minutes). If you are feeling overwhelmed, reach out for professional help (naturopath for health, child care options, government-supported respite programs, in-home nursing care). Reach out to others and avoid self-isolating. *"Many hands make light work."*

Strategies for Stress Management

1. Start by making a list of your stressors and put them into categories:

A. Situational or B. Chronic and Ongoing.

2. Make a plan. Besides each stressor, write how you can resolve it (if possible) or who you may ask to help (a professional or support person).

3. Begin building a support system; reach out to people and begin to gather them around you as your team of "cheerleaders." This could be family, close friends, your church or small group, or a local support group of people dealing with the same issue. Research shows that stress increases when we are isolated and alone but decreases when we have a support system to share our burdens.

4. Discover what you require to calm your stress. Here are some suggestions; write down the ones that stand out. Then, plan how you could incorporate them into your life.

   - Meditation, prayer, practicing thankfulness
   - Daily walk through nature
   - Exercise (walk, bike, hike, swim)
   - Hot bubble bath with candles
   - Watch comedies or listen to comedic podcasts (laughter is great medicine).

- Listen to upbeat music and dance like no one's watching.
- Take a short nap.
- Practice yoga, tai chi.
- Sauna or hot tub
- Crafts or hobbies
- Get fancy at dinner time (even if you live alone), make a nice dinner, put candles on the table, put a hand-picked flower on it, and put on soft music. Enjoy your meal; you deserve it!
- Weekly coffee with a friend
- Walk barefoot on the beach.

5. Things you need to avoid if you are stressed. Get off your social media/phone and begin living in the real world. Research shows that the more time you spend on your phone, the more you are prone to isolation and depression. Did you know that just hearing the voice of a loved one or looking into their eyes when talking face to face can be instantly calming? Find that person who calms you.

6. Follow my 4 Keys to Health. 1. Whole fresh foods (clean eating), 2. Exercise, 3. Stress management, and 4. Proper sleep. When you are eating clean, exercising, and getting appropriate amounts of sleep, your cortisol levels will automatically decrease.

Conclusion: We need to take control of our stress and stop it from controlling us. Stress can be controlled, and once again, it falls on us to take responsibility for our health.

There is a lot we can do to manage our stress, but we can't wait for someone to do it for us. Just like eating or exercising, it is up to us as individuals to reach out for help and make those changes.

Sleep: Why Sleep is Vital to Both Our Health and Longevity

We have all had that night where we couldn't sleep, maybe more than one night. The following morning, your brain is foggy, you can't concentrate, your stomach feels ill, and your energy level is nonexistent, like actors from "The Walking Dead." Seeing the effects of lack of sleep for one or two nights can give you a glimpse into how vital sleep is for our body to function.

When you sleep, your body is working to heal and store your brain function. It's even more essential for children and teens because sleep supports their growth and development. We often forget that and get into the habit of late nights followed by early mornings. Within a few short months, this could begin to cause damage to our system.

What happens to our body when we sleep?

When you are deep into your sleep, your body repairs cells, muscles, and organs. Chemicals that strengthen your immune system begin to travel through your blood. Your brain stores new information and rids itself of toxic waste.

Nerve cells communicate and reorganize to improve brain function. The body repairs cells, recharges its energy levels, and releases hormones and proteins. There is a lot of activity going on inside our bodies as we sleep!

Let's look at the parts of the body that are most affected by sleep:

1. A well-rested brain aids in the following: creativity, concentration, focus, learning, memory, problem-solving, and decision-making. Sleep increases each area of our brain: the amygdala, striatum, hippocampus, insula, and medial prefrontal cortex. A lack of sleep will affect each area of our brain.

2. A well-rested brain gives us energy and increases our metabolism. When we sleep, we conserve energy to recharge it the following day, similar to charging our cell phone. Sleeping well at night increases our metabolism during the day. If you are sleeping, you are not eating, so you are allowing your digestive system to rest and your organs to recharge. People who don't sleep well are more sluggish during the day because their metabolism (your body's engine) is revving too low. This will contribute to weight gain.

3. Sleeping well restores our cells, repairs muscle, increases protein synthesis, causes tissue growth, and balances hormones.

4. Sleeping properly helps us with weight management. When you sleep, your Leptin and Ghrelin levels are controlled. As you sleep, Ghrelin

decreases (because you are not eating), and Leptin increases (because you are fasting). Also, our blood sugar levels lower when we sleep because we are fasting. You can see why eating close to bedtime or eating in the middle of the night is going to be a problem. When you get up at two in the morning for that piece of cheesecake, you are raising insulin and increasing Ghrelin, and your body will no longer be resting. This will rev up your metabolism and will affect your sleep. People who eat just before bed or are night snackers will put on weight much quicker. This could lead to obesity, insulin resistance, metabolic syndrome, or type two diabetes.

5. Sleep affects our immune system. Recent research shows that sleep deprivation can slow our body's immune response, making us more susceptible to germs. When we sleep, our body creates cytokines. Cytokines are part of our body's defense system. These are proteins that fight both infection and inflammation within our body. When we are sleep-deprived, our body does not produce as many cytokines. This will weaken our defense system and leave us prone to illness.

6. Sleep affects our heart health. The CDC (Centers for Disease Control) recommends 7-8 hours of sleep a night for optimum health. When you are short-changing your sleep consistently, it can impact your heart. A consistent lack of sleep can cause the following:

    - Elevated cortisol levels
    - High blood pressure
    - Increased blood sugar levels

- Increased activity in the sympathetic nervous system
- Increased inflammation
- Insulin resistance
- Obesity.

Each one of these issues will have a direct effect on the functioning of your heart and cardiovascular system in general.

What are the important sleep protocols?

I've said it before, and I'll say it again: set yourself up for success and not failure. If you want to get a good night's sleep, here are some strategies. Take a look at the list below to see if there are any ideas you may be able to incorporate into your sleep protocol.

1. Start during the day. Eat properly, avoid processed foods, stay hydrated, and avoid coffee or stimulants after noon if you can.

2. Be consistent with your sleep schedule. If at all possible, wake up at the same time and go to bed at the same time. If you wake up early (with the sun) and go to bed before 10 pm (with the moon), you will set your circadian rhythm to nature.

3. Avoid eating two to three hours before bed so you are not digesting while trying to sleep. Your organs need that break to recover.

4. Avoid stimulating sounds and lights two hours before bed. Dim the lights, lower the volume of your TV, play soft music, and get off your cell phone/social media/computer. Technology is very stimulating.

5. Begin to relax before bed. Try stretching, meditation/prayer, or reading a book before bed. Light candles or set mood lighting. Take a hot bubble bath with Epsom salts and soak your body to relax. Sip some chamomile tea while in the bath.

6. Keep your bedroom dark, cool, uncluttered and comfortable.

7. Try to avoid alcohol (or sugar) before bed. Alcohol might help you to initially relax, but it definitely will disrupt your sleep. Remember, both alcohol and sugar are very hard on the liver. When your body is trying to rest and regenerate, these substances will disrupt sleep by forcing the liver (and other organs) to work instead of rest. Also, both alcohol and sugar increase blood sugar levels (and Ghrelin), which will stop your body from entering into its reparative stage.

8. Once in bed, avoid having technology in the room; it should be peaceful. Leave your cell phone charging in another room.

10. If you tossing and turning, get out of bed and read or listen to soft music. Once again, avoid technology due to its stimulating effects. Try to avoid eating; instead, have some herbal tea such as chamomile, lavender, or lemon balm. Once you feel sleepy again, try going back to bed.

These are the sleep protocols that I discuss with my clients, and most people can set up a sleep routine that works for them. However, some have some serious issues sleeping. People with insomnia or continual disruptive sleep issues should seek out an evaluation from a reputable sleep assessment clinic.

Herbal Sleep Remedies

Many herbal remedies and supplements can aid your sleep issues before you turn to prescription drugs. However, I strongly advise you to consult a naturopath, medical phytotherapist, or a health care provider before self-prescribing any herb or supplement. You will need to have them assess your nutrition, lifestyle, current medications (for contraindications), and medical conditions. There can be many reasons for insomnia, and you don't want to be guessing at what's going on and what to take.

These are some of the herbs and supplements I have recommended in the past only after we have exhausted all the nutritional and lifestyle changes necessary.

Supplements: Melatonin, Magnesium, L-Theanine, 5-HTP, and Gaba

Teas: Chamomile, Valerian, Lavender, Lemon Balm, California Poppy

Summary of Chapter 13

There are four keys to good health: whole fresh food, exercise, stress management, and proper sleep. As I said earlier, your body requires all four components to stay healthy and balanced. Here are the takeaways from this chapter:

1. When it comes to food, you should be eating fresh and local whole foods. Skip the sugar, junk food, and ultra-processed food. Remember to source your fruits and vegetables fresh and in season; always purchase Canadian (local when possible) meats and dairy. Prepare and cook your foods, so you know the quality.
2. Exercise is vital. Your exercise program should include the following: cardio, weight resistance, balance, and stretching. Aim for 30 minutes of movement a day.
3. Stress management is essential for your body and brain health. There is acute stress, which is short-term or situational. There is also chronic stress, which can be long-term or unchangeable. We discussed strategies for both and how to put a plan together to lower your stress levels.
4. Sleep is the time our body can reset and heal. We need 7 to 8 hours of sleep a night to recharge. We discussed sleep protocols and touched on herbs and supplements used as sleep aids.

Takeaway from Chapter 13:

Our bodies are both complex and wonderfully designed. It's not enough just to eat well; we must also use the three other keys. We need to move daily, relax daily, and sleep nightly. When all four components are in place, we will be in balance. It's within the balance of all four of these keys that we will find maximum health.

The 4 Keys to Health: Food, Exercise, Stress Management, and Sleep

Chapter 14
The Most Common Diets and Who Should Follow Them:
Mediterranean, Paleo (low carb), Keto, Carnivore, Vegetarian/Vegan

In the previous chapter, we discussed the North American food pyramids and why their one-size-fits-all approach is not functional. As a nutritionist, part of my job is to compile a complete medical history of my client, which includes examining lab results, vitamin and mineral deficiencies or excesses, family history, current medical issues, food intolerances, current medications/supplements and lifestyle choices (sleep, smoking, alcohol, drugs). Once I have a clear map of the client's needs, we can put together a meal plan that will best suit their own body's needs.

I'll give you an example of why one way of eating cannot work for everyone. Many members of my family have a tough time digesting grains and legumes. Some are intolerant, others have severe allergies, and a few are Celiac. However, most of us have the LCT gene that can digest dairy well; we thrive on it. We also do very well with all animal proteins, vegetables, and small amounts of fruits.

When I followed the Canada Food Guide (1990) to try and lose weight (as per my hospital dietician), I was constantly bloated and gassy and daily struggled with headaches and inflammation. When I finally went onto Atkin's Diet low carb diet, I cut out all grains, sugar, and starches. Within two weeks, everything appeared to clear up. That low-carb diet was a type of elimination diet, clearing me from all the allergy-triggering foods. Since 1992, I have followed a strict ketogenic diet, stayed at a BMI of 21-22, and I am still feeling amazing. Keto works wonderfully for me but may not work for everyone.

Part of being a good nutritionist is being able to properly investigate clients while also knowing the foods that match their individual needs. Over the years, I have recommended the Mediterranean diet, the Paleo diet, the Ketogenic diet, the Carnivore diet, and, in very rare circumstances, the Vegetarian/Vegan diet with heavy supplementation. But in no way would I recommend that every person on the planet follow one specific way of eating.

In this chapter, we will examine each of the various eating styles of eating; Mediterranean, Paleo, Keto, Carnivore, Vegetarian, and Vegan. We will also consider who would benefit most from each diet and why. At the start of each one, I provide a client example to make it practical.

Mediterranean Diet

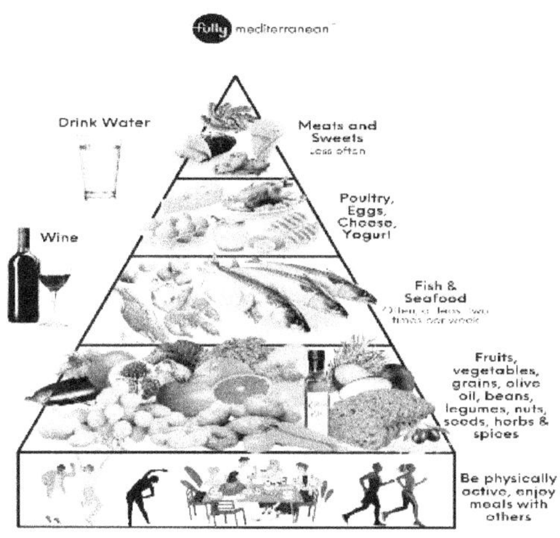

Basis:

The Mediterranean diet follows both the lifestyle and foods eaten by people living along the shores of the Mediterranean Sea. They live a very wholesome and relaxed lifestyle. The focus is on local and in-season fresh fruits, vegetables, fresh fish, olives, olive oil and some dairy. The Mediterranean's predominantly cook at home and enjoy sharing meals with others. The family meal is crucial to them. Like people in France, they are very active, eat smaller amounts of food, and use mealtime to gather and socialize. The community is close-knit, and they focus on family connections.

If you notice the pyramid above, its foundation is exercise and movement. I long for the day we see this as the foundation of our North American food pyramids! I would add sleep and stress management to this foundation as well.

Let's take a closer look at what the Mediterraneans eat.

- The main foods they consume are: fish and all forms of seafood, meat, and poultry (a few times a week), fresh fruits and vegetables, small amounts of dairy (especially yogurt), olives/olive oil, whole grains, legumes, nuts, and seeds, healthy fats, a variety of herbs and spices, and a daily glass of red wine.
- They tend to avoid are as follows; processed meats, heavily processed foods, refined grains, hard alcohol, junk food, sugar, and refined/processed/hydrogenated oils.

Client:

One of my clients, PX1 (age 30), came to me very underweight and was struggling with fertility issues and a complete lack of appetite (low Ghrelin serum levels). She previously had an eating disorder (anorexia nervosa) but was currently in remission. She was lactose intolerant but had no other food sensitivities. She struggled with eating meat, she disliked the taste and texture but enjoyed chicken and fish. Due to the previous eating disorder, she would only eat a few bits while standing up instead of sitting for a meal. PX1 did not enjoy eating and had an unhealthy relationship with food.

She enjoyed cooking and baking and wanted to focus on eating whole, fresh food to regain her health. The client was excited about discovering new recipes. I presented her with the Mediterranean diet, where she could eat the foods she loved and experiment with new exotic recipes. There were no restrictions on how much food she could eat. I asked her to sit down to eat three times a day, even if she could only have a few bites, just to begin to trigger her appetite.

I advised her to work towards developing a loving relationship with her food. I encouraged her to prepare it with love and set a nice table for her and her family. I asked that she eat slowly, really enjoy the tastes and textures, and converse with the family while enjoying every bite. We also worked on why she was worthy of being healthy and enjoying life to its fullest.

After a couple of months, her appetite slowly began to return, and she began putting on weight. The client still follows the Mediterranean diet, focusing on home cooking, and still eats with the family. She had a son three years ago and is doing well.

Benefits:

There are many benefits of the Mediterranean diet:

- Lowers your risk of cardiovascular disease (heart attack/stroke)

- Assists in both weight maintenance and weight gain
- Maintains healthy blood sugar levels
- Regulates blood pressure and cholesterol levels
- Lowers your risk of insulin resistance and metabolic syndrome
- Promotes good gut flora, improving your digestive system
- Lowers your risk of cancer
- Lowers your risk of dementia (Alzheimer's)
- Contributes to longevity

I would recommend the Mediterranean diet for any child, teen, or healthy adult free from wheat/grain sensitivities, digestive issues, or legume allergies. It can also be easily modified for those who want to gain weight or very active or athletic people who are committed to eating a whole foods diet. This can be a good "foundational diet" for many.

Paleo Diet (Low Carb/Caveman)

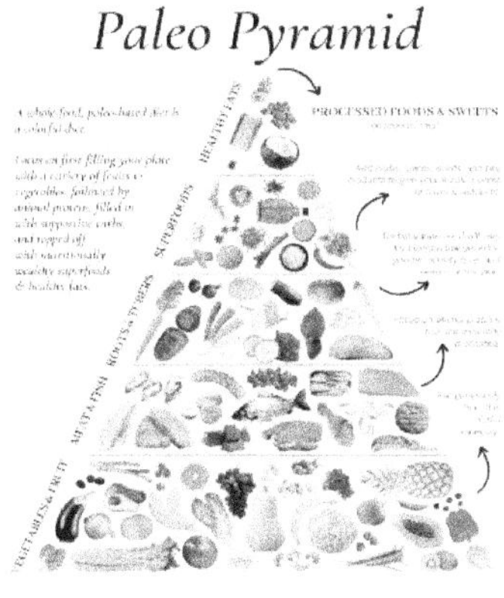

Basis:

The Paleo diet is a low-carb, high-protein diet that focuses solely on whole fresh fruits and vegetables, animal fats and proteins, eggs, nuts, and seeds. This program omits all dairy and grains. The concept of this way of eating is that these were the foods of our original ancestors before the agricultural revolution. Paleo encourages daily exercise and other appropriate wellness practices. Similar to the Mediterranean diet, Paleo focuses on local, fresh, whole foods and the elimination of sugar and ultra-processed foods.

If you look at the food pyramid above, you will notice that the foundation is fresh fruits and vegetables (not grains like the Canada Food Guide). The second level is then animal products, followed by the third level of root vegetables and tubers. The fourth level is superfoods like seeds, honey, and various herbs. The fifth level is healthy fats like coconut, nuts, seeds, and olive oil. Very well laid out as an excellent food pyramid suitable for the majority of people, especially for those having issues with grains and legumes.

The main foods consumed are as follows:

- Leafy vegetables
- Fresh fruit
- Seafood
- Grass-fed meat
- Root vegetables
- Free-range poultry
- Eggs
- Nuts and seeds
- Butter
- Healthy oils (olive oil, avocado oil, flaxseed oil, coconut oil),
- Fresh or dried herbs
- Water
- Herbal teas

Occasional foods to add in are as follows:

- Honey
- Molasses
- Dates
- Coffee

- Beer
- Wine
- Almond flour and Coconut flour for baking.

The foods to avoid are as follows:

- All grains (wheat, oats, pasta, cereal, rice)
- Dairy products (cheese, milk, and yogurt)
- All legumes (beans, peanuts, and soy)
- Potatoes (except sweet potatoes)
- All fruit and vegetable juices
- All processed foods
- All refined vegetable oils
- All added sugar
- Poor quality salt (iodized salt).

Client:

Client PX2, a male of 67 years of age, came to me with a diagnosis of both confirmed Celiac disease and anemia. He had chronic diarrhea with frequent bouts of constipation. He also suffered from chronic fatigue, gas and bloating, and severe weight loss. His Celiac symptoms were so severe he was not able to leave his home for any lengthy periods due to the chronic diarrhea. This was significantly affecting his marriage and life as a whole.

PX2 was receiving fecal transplants and had been asked

by his medical provider to seek out a holistic nutritionist to assist him with a complimentary nutritional plan. Once we went through his full assessment I recommended he follow a strict Paleo diet. I further recommended no beer or corn as well. I also increased his intake of animal protein, especially red meats and organ meats (beef liver). I explained how to cook meat properly to absorb more heme iron. I asked PX2 to eat several small meals a day and eat until he was full. Slowly, he began increasing his weight while decreasing his symptoms (diarrhea). He used nuts and seeds, along with one avocado a day, as a snack to increase his caloric intake. I took coffee out of his diet, and we worked on a new sleep routine alongside an easy-to-follow exercise program.

Within three months his symptoms had began to decrease. He was able to go grocery shopping and go out to dinner without symptoms arising. He had put on a few pounds and was sleeping better. He felt like he was getting his life back. This client did amazing on Paleo!

Benefits:

These are the benefits of the Paleo diet:

- Decreases the risk of cardiovascular disease
- Lowers blood sugar levels (lowering the risk of insulin resistance and diabetes)
- It is an anti-inflammatory diet
- Improves sleep

- Improves skin (eczema and acne)
- Improves mental clarity
- Increases immune system
- Improves symptoms of autoimmune disorders/autism and ADHD
- Increases energy

I would recommend the Paleo diet for the following clients:

Children with autism and ADHD, people with celiac disease/non-celiac disease, IBS, wheat and gluten allergies, lactose intolerance, obesity, cardiovascular disease, metabolic syndrome, or those who have lost weight and would like to maintain that weight. Many of my clients have also chosen this way of eating because they want to simply "eat clean," and it makes them feel better mentally and physically.

Ketogenic Diet (Similar To Atkins)

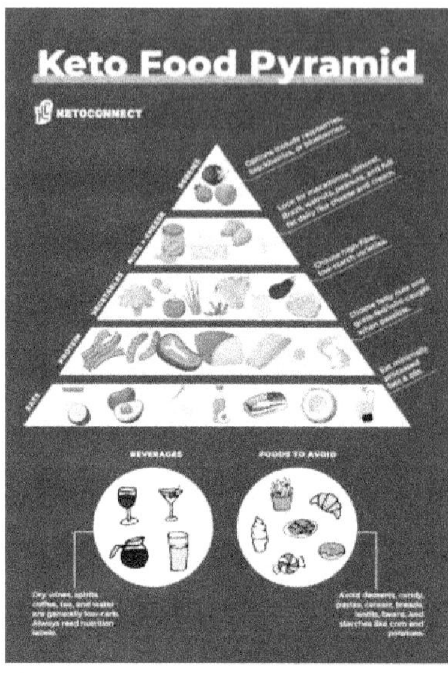

The Ketogenic diet is a high-fat, moderate protein, very low-carb diet that causes the body to break down fat into molecules called ketones. The body can use two types of fuel, either carbohydrates or fat. Most people follow diets high in carbohydrates (sugar, grains, oats, pasta, rice, breads, ultra-processed foods, and desserts). Those carbohydrates will fuel your bodily functions (brain, organs, and metabolism). A high-carb diet increases both insulin and increases Ghrelin. Think of carbohydrates as gas for your car.

Now your body can also use fat as a very efficient fuel, even more efficient than carbs. When you are on a ketogenic diet, your body begins burning fat as fuel; this creates "ketones." This "fat fuel" is a much cleaner burn and greatly increases your energy levels (fat and protein increase Leptin). When your body uses fat/ketones as fuel, it is similar to using diesel in your car.

Think back to when we talked about organs and hormones. The hormone Ghrelin (which is turned on by carbohydrates) increases your appetite and raises your blood sugar levels. On the ketogenic diet, you are increasing the hormone Leptin, the satiating hormone. When you increase fat and protein while lowering carbohydrates, you will decrease your appetite.

Important Note:

Although your body can use either carbs or fat as fuel sources, you must not use both fuels at the same time! You can cause damage to your organs by eating a high-carb diet along with a high-fat diet. This could cause cardiovascular issues, hormonal issues, and liver issues, opening you up to metabolic syndrome, diabetes, and NAFLD. Similar to what would happen if you pull up to the gas station and put both diesel and gas in your tank at the same time.

So, if you are on a high-carb diet try removing all the ultra-processed foods and all sugar out of your diet and lower your calorie intake. On a high-carb diet, do not increase your fat. But if you are on a keto/low-carb diet, then increase your fats, keep proteins moderate, and eat lots of buttered vegetables. Remember to keep your carbs under 30 grams a day. Whatever fuel you choose to use, keep the same fuel in your tank. By the way, all the diseases you are seeing today are due to our country's high-carb diet mixed with poor-quality fats (seed oils, vegetable oils, canola oil, trans fats). Our current "recommended" North American diet uses both fuels, which is why you are seeing all the various health issues arising.

The ketogenic diet was discovered by Russell Wilder, M.D. (The Mayo Clinic) on July 27, 1921. His discovery of the ketogenic diet was based on the theory that a high-fat, very low-carb diet (using fat as a fuel, producing ketones) could be as effective as fasting, leading to the treatment of epileptic seizures. The Mayo Clinic then tested the theory on both children and adults with epilepsy, and it was shown to be a great success.

The ketogenic diet is currently being used by other medical institutions (including Johns Hopkins and the Mayo Clinic). The KD (Ketogenic Diet) has been implemented worldwide in 73 academic centers in 41 countries outside the United States. Keto has not only been used for epileptic seizures but also shows promise in helping to treat the following:

- Insulin resistance
- Metabolic syndrome
- NAFLD

- Autism,
- Diabetes
- ADHD,
- Autoimmune disorders
- Dementia/Alzheimer's
- Some forms of cancer

The ketogenic diet recommends eating whole foods and fresh when possible. There is no counting calories but carbohydrates should be kept at under 30 grams a day. Having said that, some people who can metabolize carbs well can still maintain ketosis at 50 carbs.

The main foods consumed on the ketogenic diet are as follows:

- Fish, seafood, poultry, pork, lamb, goat, beef etc
- Low-carb veggies (all low-carb vegetables are free to eat - add coconut oil or butter for better absorption)
- Dairy (full-fat cheese, sour cream, cream, cheese, full-fat plain yogurt)
- Avocados
- Eggs
- Nuts and seeds
- Good fats (olive oil, coconut oil, avocado oil, grass-fed butter, ghee, lard, tallow)
- Baking made with almond flour, coconut flour, eggs, full-fat milk, stevia is acceptable

- Fruits: small amounts of berries (blackberries, blueberries, strawberries), lemons/limes
- Unsweetened coffee, tea, herbal teas
- Natural Sweeteners (raw organic stevia, organic monk fruit)
- Bitter dark chocolate and cocoa powder (85% and up)
- All dried herbs and spices, vanilla for baking
- Lots of clean water (add electrolyte powder)

The main foods to avoid on the ketogenic diet are as follows:

- Grains/starches (bread, pasta, rice, oats)
- Legumes and beans (string beans are fine)
- Sugar (desserts, junk food, candy, sweets, honey, all other sugar products)
- Ultra-processed foods
- High-carb fruits (keep at the lowest end of the glycemic index and no juicing)
- Starchy vegetables (potatoes, yams, corn, taro root)
- Low fat/ no fat dairy (remember low fat or no fat contains sugar or sugar substitutes and is ultra-processed)
- Diet or sugar-free products
- Trans fat and hydrogenated oil (E.g., margarine, vegetable shortening, commercial cakes, cookies, microwave popcorn, and frozen pizza)

Client:

Client PX3 was a Jamaican-decent female (age 45) having both medical issues and difficult peri-menopausal symptoms. She had put on 40 lbs since her hormones had begun fluctuating. She had also been diagnosed with NAFLD (elevated ALT), elevated A1C (pre-diabetic), gradual weight gain, and difficulty sleeping due to night sweats.

This woman consumed a high-carb/low-fat diet (much of her food was ultra-processed). The staples of her diet were various grains, rice and peas, tubers, Jamaican dumplings, Jamaican patties, cassava, fried plantain, and lots of very sweet fruit. She enjoyed a variety of vegetables and loved her cultural dishes (fish soup, curried goat, jerk chicken, and beef).

When she arrived in Canada, she began buying all low-fat products (low-fat dairy and low-fat cheese/ yogurt, low-fat desserts, Becel margarine, and vegetable oil to cook with). Under the advice of her nurse, who had told her that to lose weight, she should cut fat from her diet, stop eating meat, and stick to fish while increasing carbohydrates. PX3 complied, and two years later, she was feeling worse and was 40 lbs heavier.

While living in Jamaica, she could metabolize the carbs better because she was eating mostly whole foods, and fresh fruits and veg in season. She would also walk everywhere She was quite active. However, once she came to Canada and entered peri-menopause, she began to quickly put on weight and was dealing with many metabolic illnesses (pre-diabetes and NAFLD). She was already interested in Keto because a co-worker had been successful at losing weight and lowering her A1C on that diet.

I worked with this client to formulate a ketogenic program that fit her cultural needs as well as her medical needs. We even found a site that formatted traditional recipes into keto-friendly recipes (Keto Diet for the Caribbean & Beyond). She was able to adapt to keto completely and enjoyed experimenting with new cultural recipes. She began walking with her friend, and they supported each other. PX3 is at her goal weight, is sleeping well (also due to a new sleep protocol), her liver markers (Alt) and glucose levels (A1C) are now within the normal range, and she is feeling better. When she went back home to Jamaica for a recent visit, people were shocked to see how well she looked. This gave her a great confidence boost!

Benefits:

As a nutritionist, I have seen many improvements in patients who choose to follow the ketogenic diet. I have also seen huge shifts in my own health on keto. I've been on a very low carb/no sugar or processed food diet since 1992/93.

At 58 years old, my health is excellent, and I take no medications. I sailed through menopause and have an abundance of energy. I continue to work out 3-4 times a week. In my opinion, having extra energy, feeling great, and looking good for my chronological age is a benefit in itself. Research is telling us there are far more possible benefits to the ketogenic diet. I draw your attention to a recent research paper published in PubMed Central(May 13, 2021) in which the authors investigate the benefits of the ketogenic diet.

PubMed Central, May 13, 2021 (PMCID: PMC8153354), "The Potential Health Benefits of the Ketogenic Diet: A Narrative Review written by Kathryn Dowis and Simran Banga.

Ketogenic diets have started to increase in popularity as doctors and researchers investigate the potential benefits. Nutritional ketosis, the aspirational endpoint of ketogenic diets, is achieved by restricting carbohydrate intake, moderating protein consumption, and increasing the number of calories obtained from fat [1]. Theoretically, this restriction of carbohydrates causes the body to switch from glucose metabolism as a primary means of energy production. This results in the use of ketone bodies from fat metabolism, a metabolic state where the body prefers to utilize fat as its primary fuel source. Recent studies utilizing Low-carbohydrate, High-fat (LCHF) diets, such as the ketogenic diet, show promise in helping patients lose weight, reverse the signs of metabolic syndrome, reduce or eliminate insulin requirements for type II diabetics [2], reduce inflammation, improve epigenetic profiles, alter the microbiome, improve lipid profiles, supplement cancer treatments, and potentially increase longevity [3] and brain function. (Dowis K, 2021)

The list of benefits for those who have both the ability and desire to follow a ketogenic diet has been well documented and researched. The ketogenic diet may be well suited for those who are dealing with the following:

- Obesity
- Insulin resistance
- Metabolic syndrome
- Type 2 Diabetes
- NAFLD
- Inflammation
- High blood pressure
- Heart (general health)
- Elevated Triglycerides
- Autoimmune diseases
- Arthritis (OA and RA)
- Epilepsy
- Alzheimers/Dementia
- Autism/ADHA/AuDHA
- Cancer

- Mental illness (schizophrenia/bipolar/depression/anxiety)

As always, I would recommend people who are interested in trying keto to see a certified nutritionist or naturopath first who is well-trained in the ketogenic diet specifically. We always want to go over people's health profiles first before recommending any diet; remember that people are all unique. There are several ways of individually adapting the keto diet for almost anyone. Many holistic nutritionists, naturopaths, and doctors have training in the ketogenic diet specifically. I give this diet an A+ rating for those who are formatted to it.

Carnivore Diet

What is this new "meat diet" that we are hearing so much about? The carnivore diet consists of eating only meat and animal products (meat, poultry, seafood, animal fat, eggs, dairy) with the exclusion of all other food groups. The carnivore diet is often used as a strict elimination diet.

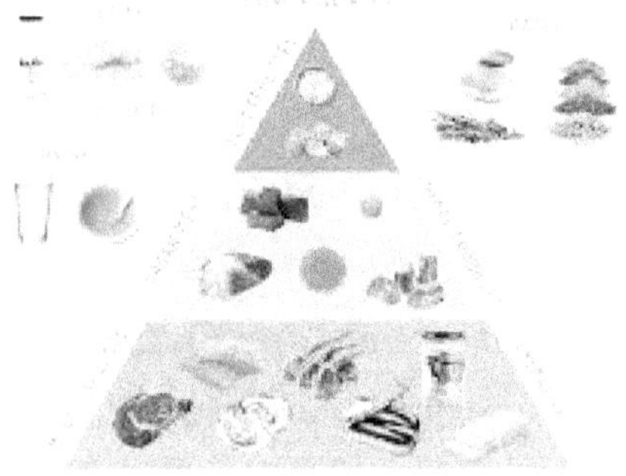

Basis:

Where did this "all-meat diet" originate from? The Carnivore diet came onto the scene in 1856 when German writer Bernard Moncriff (author of The Philosophy of the Stomach) spent a year consuming only beef and milk. His health flourished and he felt he had stumbled onto a new and improved way of eating.

Then, in 1870, an Italian physician (Dr. Arnoldo Cantani) began prescribing his diabetic patients an all-animal protein-based diet as a form of treatment. He saw significant improvements in his patients.

In 1880, an American physician (Dr. James Henry Salisbury) came up with "The Salisbury Diet" as a 4 to 12-week type of elimination diet. This 4 to 12-week diet consisted of 2 to 4 pounds of beef and 3 to 5 pints (5-6 litres) of hot water a day. Again, he saw some excellent results with his patient base.

In 2018, an Orthopedic surgeon/world-renowned athlete (Dr. Shawn Baker) wrote the book "The Carnivore Diet." The concept is that by eating a strict animal-based diet, patients would lower their inflammatory markers, decreasing pain and being able to avoid unnecessary surgery. This appeared to work for most patients, including himself.

Dr. Baker wrote the "Carnivore diet book" after years of witnessing the failure of the mainstream healthcare system to prevent and effectively treat numerous epidemic chronic diseases (joint pain, type 2 diabetes, obesity, heart disease, and cancer). He was seeing many patients come in for surgery who could have avoided surgery intervention if they had changed their diet.

More recently, Canadian Psychologist (Jordan Peterson) and his daughter Mikhaila Peterson (YouTuber) both had rather miraculous health recoveries after adhering to a strict carnivore diet. Jordan Peterson suffered from mental health issues and severe benzodiazepine withdrawal syndrome, and he experienced healing for both after changing his diet to carnivore (he later coined "The Lion Diet"). Jordan's daughter, Mikhaila, has juvenile idiopathic arthritis (an autoimmune disease). After months on a carnivore diet, she saw her symptoms reverse, and she is now a huge supporter of the Carnivore/Lion diet for autoimmune diseases.

The main foods consumed on a Carnivore diet are as follows:

- Meat: beef, lamb, pork, game, chicken, turkey, organ meats etc.
- Fish: salmon, tuna, mackerel, sardines, crab, etc.
- Animal Products: eggs, bone marrow, lard, bone broth, etc.
- Dairy products (in small amounts): butter, heavy cream, hard cheese, etc.
- Seasonings (with no carbs): salt, black pepper, etc.
- Water

The main foods to avoid on a Carnivore diet are as follows:

- All Fruits
- All Vegetables
- All Grains
- High-lactose dairy: soft cheese, milk, yogurt
- All Legumes:
- All Nuts and seeds:
- Alcohol: beer, wine, liquor
- All Sugars: (sugar, honey, maple syrup)
- Beverages other than water: coffee, soda, tea, juice

Client:

PX4 is a female (age 24) who was diagnosed with both rheumatoid arthritis (autoimmune disease) and Crohn's disease. She was suffering from joint pain, chronic diarrhea, chronic fatigue, brain fog, and frequent headaches. This client has several family members with various food intolerances and allergies, so I requested for her to get further testing.

I wanted her to try a ketogenic diet, but due to the level of suffering she was experiencing, I wanted her to try a strict elimination diet first. We went with the carnivore diet with the aim of eight weeks to see if symptoms improved until we had further results of food sensitivities. After four weeks, she saw a vast improvement in her joint pain, and the diarrhea had ceased. She was starting to sleep better at night, her energy had greatly improved, and she was feeling much better.

By week eight, the food allergy testing had revealed she also had dairy sensitivity and nonceliac gluten sensitivity. Once we had all the information, I recommended the ketogenic diet with the removal of dairy. I will note the client had no issues with fermented dairy (yogurt and kefir), so I kept them in for gut health. At this point, PX4 was feeling much better and was feeling as if she was getting her life back. She chose to remain on the Carnivore diet and remains symptom-free today.

Benefits:

Currently, studies are being conducted on the Carnivore diet (aka All Meat diet, Salisbury diet, the Lion diet). Researchers are studying various people groups who have traditionally eaten an all-meat-based diet: the Canadian Inuit, the Russian Chukotka, and the African tribes (Masai, Samburu, and Rendille). Having said that, there appear to be consistent results showing the Carnivore diet is effective in weight loss, improving autoimmune symptoms, identifying food sensitivities, and resetting the body from the effects of a high-carb diet. This diet is an anti-inflammatory diet in the true sense. As a nutritionist, I do see room to use this diet, at least on a short-term basis. When something is working for clients, and you can see them thriving in their lives as well as their lab results improving, healthcare professionals must stand up and take notice.

Vegetarian/Vegan Diet (AKA Plant-Based)

The thing I appreciate about both the vegetarian diet and the vegan diet is the removal of all junk food and ultra-processed foods. People who are trying to follow this way of eating are taking charge of their health by being very aware of the foods they are choosing to consume. In our current day and age, major corporations are trying to convince us to eat food that is ultra-processed, sugar-filled, and made with poor-quality fats, various dyes, fillers, and chemicals. When I see people striving to change that way of thinking and begin to make steps towards consuming a whole foods diet (fresh and local foods) and a healthy lifestyle, I commend them greatly!

I do believe that a strict vegetarian or vegan diet is only applicable to a very select few. Most will not do well on either of these diets and they include the following:

- Our First Nations people
- Those with anemia
- Those who have wheat (gluten) allergies/sensitivities
- Those with Celiac disease
- Autoimmune diseases
- Those with legume sensitivities
- Diabetics
- Those with vitamin D and vitamin K deficiencies

Mind you, this is the shortlist.

I have seen too many vegetarian/vegan clients who are weak, anemic, suffer hair loss, and muscle loss, are infertile, depressed, and are vitamin/mineral deficient. The increased grains, legumes, ultra-processed vegan products (fake meats/fake cheeses), the high consumption of soy products, and an overabundance of fruits (especially juiced) can harm the body.

The biggest issue with plant-based diets is the lack of animal protein (heme protein). We already spoke about the importance of heme protein (animal products in general), which builds blood, increases muscle mass, increases brain function, and balances hormones to increase Leptin (controls hunger), hair, and nails.

Basis of the Vegetarian and Vegan Diets

Here are the definitions of vegan and various vegetarian diets:

- The lactovegetarian diet includes plant foods plus dairy products.
- The lacto-ovo-vegetarian diet consists of both dairy products and eggs.
- The Pescatarian diet is all plant-based, with seafood as the source of protein.
- The vegan diet includes only plant foods and excludes all meat and animal products, including eggs.

Client:

PX5 is a male truck driver (age 52) recently diagnosed with hemochromatosis. Hemochromatosis is a genetic disorder in which the body stores and holds onto iron, causing an iron overload. The iron accumulates in various organs (liver, pancreas, thyroid, heart, pituitary, joints, skin, and gonads) and causes organ damage via oxidative stress.

Those with hemochromatosis are asked to give blood frequently to decrease their iron levels.

PX5 had symptoms of fatigue, depression, joint pain in the hands, and erectile dysfunction. The client had been eating a standard Canadian diet and frequented fast food restaurants. This client was referred for nutritional advice by his physician.

PX5 was placed on a pescatarian/vegetarian diet. He was struggling to give up animal protein, so we settled on allowing fish in small amounts twice a week. The majority of his diet was vegetables (both cooked and raw), 3-4 whole fruits a day, baked yams with a little coconut oil daily, one large avocado daily, ancient grains (bread and products), black wild rice, pre-soaked legumes, steel cut oats, mixtures of nuts and seeds for snacks on the road.

We removed junk food, ultra-processed food, and pop from his diet. We taught him how to meal prep when he was home; that way, he could bring his meals with him on the road. We also swapped the pop for ice water in a thermos with mint leaves. As a backup plan, we went over his regular fast food places to see what he could order off the menu if need be. He continued to give blood every two months.

PX5 did very well on the new pescatarian vegetarian diet. The first month was a big adjustment for him, but he developed a system that worked for him. By twelve weeks, the joint pain had lessened, he was feeling better in general, and his energy levels had increased. This client could have done well on a vegan or vegetarian diet as well.

Benefits:

Following a vegan or strict vegetarian diet will clean up your diet from ultra-processed foods and junk food. People who follow this way of eating are usually very health-conscious and have a desire to be environmentally friendly. These are very commendable reasons to take into consideration when choosing what you are going to put into your body. Any diet that does not follow the "Standard American Diet" and focuses on fresh whole foods is a better choice. However, the vast majority are not able to eat a vegan/vegetarian diet. In fact, it could be detrimental to the health of some. As a nutritionist, I only recommend this way of eating for a very select few and always with the help of supplementation of sublingual B12 and Iron infusions.

Cautions:

Both vegan and vegetarian diets can increase your risk of specific nutritional deficiencies. Our bodies require animal (heme) protein from meat, poultry, and fish for B12 and omega-3 fatty acids. Animal protein also provides us with micronutrients such as zinc, selenium, and iron. Other animal products such as dairy and eggs are excellent sources of calcium, vitamin D, and various B vitamins.

Symptoms of deficiencies on strict vegetarian/vegan diets are as follows:

- Anemia,
- Fatigue,
- Depression,
- Muscular loss and weakness,
- Weight loss (or weight gain if consuming ultra-processed foods)
- Hair loss
- Brittle nails
- Increased risk of stroke
- Risk of memory loss
- Lower bone mass density, causing a higher risk of fractures

Summary of Chapter 14

As a nutritionist, I am convinced that each person is unique and specifically designed. That being said, we can never have a one-size-fits-all nutritional approach. Some people are genetically geared to anemia and should never be placed on a vegan/vegetarian diet. There are those with autoimmune diseases or various food sensitivities and they should not be consuming a Standard American Diet (excess grains, legumes, and perhaps dairy). Then, some carry genetic mutations such as hemochromatosis and should not eat a keto or carnivore diet where animal protein is the foundational source. The list goes on.

What I really appreciate about the most "popular" forms of eating, Mediterranean, Paleo, Carnivore, Keto, and Vegan/Vegetarian, is that they all eliminate ultra-processed foods, junk foods, and sugar. The other key theme to these diets is that those people are all committing themselves to better health and are taking responsibility for their own bodies. That must be commended.

People spend a lot of time arguing over which "diet is better," and in my opinion, that is a complete waste of time. Each diet can work but must be applied to the person who requires it. That is why I encourage ALL people to sit down with a Holistic Nutritionist or a functional dietitian (open-minded) or well-trained naturopath and delve into what you require as an individual. Holistic Nutritionists are specifically trained in the science of nutrition and all of us are striving to help clients see success. I strongly suggest everyone have a CBC blood panel run (alt/ast/TSH/B12/Feratin/Kidney aldosterone/lipid panel that includes APO1). Also, request a vitamin/mineral deficiency test to assess your health; you can't take supplementation if you aren't aware of what you are deficient or in excess of. If you have genetic issues or food allergies/sensitivities that run through your family, have those tests performed as well.

People strive to gain back their health, lose weight and get into shape. All of us want to live longer, but you can't get to the end game without knowing where you are starting from. Let me explain it this way: it would be silly for you to take your car to the veterinarian. It's just as silly to ask doctors, nurses, or other practitioners for nutritional advice if that this not their scope of practice. Doctors and nurses both get an average of one course on nutrition during their many years of education. That course is often outdated. One of my associates graduated a few years ago and is a local doctor. He took one nutritional course in his first year, and the text book had information in it from 1973. Much has changed since 1973. As nutritionists, we must constantly upgrade and follow the new food science; food is our only scope of practice, so use us!

The Most Common Diets and Who Should Follow Them

Chapter 15 Intermittent Fasting

Given the popularity of "intermittent fasting," I realized I should add a chapter discussing what it is, how it works, and its importance. Intermittent fasting is an eating plan that moves between periods of eating (eating windows) and periods of not eating (fasting). Our bodies do not require to be fed on an hourly basis. Fasting between meals has been proven to have many health benefits. As we have done in previous chapters, let's look at how our great-grandparents timed their meals (their "eating window").

A 150 years ago, families would eat breakfast, lunch, and dinner three times a day. Snacks were not a regular occurrence at that time. Typically, they would eat breakfast early in the morning (5-6 am) to "break-fast" and prepare for the early morning chores. Lunch would be around noon, sometimes brought out to the fields, other times at home around the table. Dinner would usually be around 5 or 6 pm, where the whole family would gather after working for the main meal. They would get to bed early so they were not up snacking at night. They would be in bed by 8 or 9 pm to be up at dawn for morning chores. Our ancestors worked much harder physically than we do today and seemed to survive quite well without a regular intake of snacks.

Let's look at what their fasting hours would have been. Between bedtime and breakfast was about nine hours with no food. From breakfast to lunch, they would fast for about six hours. They would fast for approximately another five or six hours from lunch to dinner. Totaling the number of hours a day they would not be eating to 20 hours without food. Also, remember they were working physically harder than we do today unless you are farming or working strenuous labor.

Today, we are obsessed with eating. We have three to six meals a day, snacks regularly and we are usually not seated at a table for any of them. We eat in our car, at our desks, on the bus, and we even eat while working out. We have to pack food with us anytime we leave the house. Then there is "grazing." Some people don't "eat a meal; they just eat smaller amounts of food all day. That usually adds up to a higher quantity of food than if they would have sat down for three meals.

Did you know your organs require a break from eating to rest and repair? If you are constantly eating, you are overworking those organs. Eating continually keeps your insulin high and increases your Ghrelin hormone, making you desire more food. Fasting increases the Leptin hormone, which will decrease your desire for food. We will discuss the other medical benefits of fasting later in the chapter.

Many people claim intermittent fasting is a "new fad," but I disagree. People have been fasting for centuries. As a person of faith, I am quite familiar with fasting. Most faiths have set periods of fasting in the calendar year. Christians have a combination of prayer and fasting, Catholics have "Lent," the Jewish faith has "Yom Kippur," and Muslims have "Ramadan." These times of fasting are meant to take the focus off us and the pleasure of food and to refocus on faith. Many worldwide also use fasting as a time to cleanse the body (Buddhism). Needless to say, fasting has been around for thousands of years.

The Most Popular Types of Intermittent Fasting

Intermittent fasting can be done in many ways. You can individualize your fast to what works for you. Here are some of the most common types of intermittent fasts:

- **The fast between meals**: Here you would eat three meals a day but no snacks between those meals. Your last meal would be a few hours before sleep.
- **The 12-hour fast:** Some people hold off on breakfast until 9-11 am, so they have 12 hours between when they go to bed and when they have their first meal
- **The 14-hour fast:** You can do this by having an early dinner and then not eating until you wake up
- **The 16-hour fast:** This is my choice of intermittent fast. It works out to two meals a day. I eat a large dinner at 6 pm then my next meal is at noon (a larger lunch). I am

not a big breakfast eater, so this falls into my comfort zone.

- **The 24-hour fast (aka the OMAD - one meal a day):** This fast gives you a one-hour-per-day eating window. Some people choose lunchtime or dinnertime, eating whole fresh foods until they feel full. Their fast will then resume right after eating until the following day.
- **The 36-hour fast (aka the body reset fast):** This fast is for three days. This is usually done for medical reasons, which we will discuss later (autophagy), as a body reset, or for spiritual reasons. Many do this fast with water, herbal teas, and bone broths.

Three days to 30-day fasts are carried out by some for medical reasons. I would suggest people new to fasting not try one of these longer fasts until they are used to fasting. It would be a shock to your body. Success on these longer fasts is easier if you are already following a low-carb, carnivore, or ketogenic diet. On these diets, your Leptin hormone will function well, and you will not be as hungry. This will prepare you for longer forms of fasting. If you are following a high-carb diet (typical North American diet), your Ghrelin hormone will be high, and your insulin will fluctuate between highs and lows. This will make fasting far more difficult as you will be constantly hungry. This is why those on lower-carb diets usually follow intermittent fasting; it is easier to fast.

As a nutritionist, I am a believer in intermittent fasting. I have seen the effects on my health from clean eating and fasting. I have also seen some very real benefits of fasting in my client's health. However, I caution people to start slowly. You do not want to put unnecessary stress on your body. I always suggest clients begin slowly and work their way up to longer fasts (if they desire).

The easiest way is to try a week without snacking between meals. You should ensure your meals are nutritious and that you are having slightly larger meals.

After you are comfortable with that, try a 14 or 16-hour fast. Within a few months, you can look at the longer fasts. The key is to give your body time to adapt to fasting gently. You want to be gentle with your organs.

What can you eat and drink while doing a fast?

While you are fasting, you should not eat food. You will be relying on liquids only. Here is a list of beverages permitted on a fast: freshwater (2 to 3 liters a day); this may include mineral water, sparkling water, herbal teas, and coffee/tea with no sweeteners or cream/milk added. The idea is to avoid calories so that the body/organs can stay in a state of resting and regenerating.

If you are doing a 24-hour fast or are fasting for several days, add bone broth to your list. Bone broth (beef, chicken, fish) will give you some vital nutrients such as amino acids (proline, arginine, and glycine) and minerals: Calcium, magnesium, and phosphorus. The salt will also aid in balancing your electrolytes. and assist in hydration.

Avoid pop, diet pop, flavored coffees, canned coffee drinks, milk, energy drinks, and any types of juices (store-bought or homemade). These will move you out of your fasting state by spiking your insulin. These drinks may also increase the Ghrelin hormone, increasing your hunger and making it more challenging to commit to your fast.

How to break a long fast?

Just as important as what to consume on a fast is how to break the fast. You will want to break your fast gently. If you are just fasting between meals or doing the 12-24 hours fast, this will not be as important to adhere to. For those fasting for 36 hours or several days, you will need to break your fast slowly.

Have a meal that is composed of whole fresh foods. Eat until you are full, but don't overdo it, and avoid any fast food, greasy, or ultra-processed foods. Also, avoid anything with sugar or an overabundance of fruit, as this may cause diarrhea.

Here are some examples of gentle restarts:

- Scrambled eggs
- Hearty soups
- Meat protein
- Avocado
- Roasted vegetables

- Full-fat Greek yogurt with blueberries

Remember to eat until you are full, but don't overeat; your stomach will have shrunk a little, and you don't want to stress your system. Eating light will allow your organs to begin working again gently.

The research on Intermittent fasting

I first heard about the medical benefits of intermittent fasting from Nephrologist Dr. Jason Fung. He remains one of the top promoters of intermittent fasting today. I would encourage you to follow him on YouTube, he has a wealth of information and research on Intermittent fasting. The research today shows real promise as a medical treatment for many diseases. Studies show that intermittent fasting can be used to assist in weight loss, maintain your goal weight, and even prevent or reverse some specific diseases. Some of my clients have reversed their Type 2 diabetes using a combination of a ketogenic diet alongside intermittent fasting.

Research on Intermittent fasting by the Johns Hopkins Medicine Center

Below are direct quotes taken from the Johns Hopkins Medicine Site article:

Johns Hopkins neuroscientist Mark Mattson has studied intermittent fasting for 25 years. He says our bodies have evolved to be able to go without food for many hours or even several days or longer. In prehistoric times, before humans learned to farm, they were hunters and gatherers who evolved to survive — and thrive — for long periods without eating. They had to: It took a lot of time and energy to hunt game and gather nuts and berries."

Intermittent fasting benefits:

Research shows that the intermittent fasting periods do more than burn fat. Mattson explains, "When changes occur with this metabolic switch, it affects the body and brain."

One of Mattson's studies published in the New England Journal of Medicine revealed data about a range of health benefits associated with the practice. These include a longer life, a leaner body, and a sharper mind.

Thinking and memory. Studies discovered that intermittent fasting boosts working memory in animals and verbal memory in adult humans. Heart health. Intermittent fasting improved blood pressure and resting heart rates, as well as other heart-related measurements. Physical performance. Young men who fasted for 16 hours showed fat loss while maintaining muscle mass. Mice who were fed on alternate days showed better endurance in running. (John Hopkins Medicine , n.d.)

Autophagy

If you have read about Intermittent fasting, you will be very familiar with one of fasting's biggest benefits, autophagy. What is autophagy? Autophagy occurs when your body breaks down and reuses old cells so your new cells can operate far more efficiently. This is a natural process (occurring during long periods of fasting 24-48 hours) that begins when your cells are deprived of nutrients. To simplify, your body is getting rid of the old cells and rejuvenating new cells, thus making your body healthier. Many current research studies are being conducted on the role of autophagy in fighting specific diseases, including decreasing cancer cells.

Who should not do intermittent fasting?

Intermittent fasting is very safe for the average person. However, some should avoid fasting unless under the direct advice of a medical practitioner. These would include;

1. Children and teens under age 18
2. Women who are pregnant or breastfeeding
3. Those with type 1 diabetes who are on insulin
4. Those who have a history of eating disorders

Other than those mentioned above, I strongly suggest that those who can should give intermittent fasting a try.

Takeaway from Chapter 15

We all desire to be healthy and find the keys to longevity. Intermittent fasting can be essential to longevity, especially when accompanied by a low-carb diet that focuses on whole fresh foods.

In this chapter, we learned that Intermittent fasting has some amazing health benefits and can be fitted into almost any meal plan. Just remember to start slow, build up to longer fasts, adhere to the allowed liquids, gently come out of your fast, and enjoy the health benefits!

Intermittent Fasting

Conclusion

As the author, I want to bring you, the reader, back to why you chose this book specifically. Perhaps the title "The Corruption of Food" piqued your interest. Maybe it was the sub-title "How to win back your health?" Whatever brought you here as a reader, I can be sure you are on your journey to finding the keys to health. Perhaps you have a specific health condition you are dealing with. You may be wanting to lose weight and get back into shape. For some, you may just want to live well into your old age for your grandkids. Whatever brought you here, I applaud your search for the truth about nutrition.

We are only given one body and one life to live. How we take care of our health today will determine our elderly years, and that's important not just for ourselves but also for those who love us. We are all on a search for longevity and vitality. However, if we have longevity but are infirm and ridden with disease, we have not won the battle. Would it not be better to be able to age with fewer limitations, have a sharp mind, and be in good health? It is possible, but it begins with what you eat today.

I have always learned by example, and I'm sure you do as well. Earlier in the book, I spoke about my bodybuilding hero, Ernestine Shepherd. At age 86, she still competed in bodybuilding for her age category. Her commitment to healthy eating and her dedication to exercise inspired me to do the same in my late fifties. This is who I want to be in my eighties!

Last year, we buried my husband's father in Jamaica, Vincent Robinson. Vincent died at the age of 106. Until that day, he sang hymns, played the harmonica, went to church with the family, fed himself, and laughed a lot. He was very active. He kept working around the yard into his 90s and ate three square meals daily. Those meals included traditional Jamaican dishes, meat, vegetables, and fruit. He never smoked or drank alcohol. He was another example of how to live a good and healthy life.

Over the last fifteen chapters, we discussed practical ways to regain health. Let's do a quick recap of what we have learned together. We began with our ancestors' history, which led us to realize how our food system became corrupted over time. We covered new and disturbing "food-caused" diseases that our great-grandparents never had to deal with. That led us to a deep dive into every food group and the need to keep hydrated. We also spoke about the harms of sugar and ultra-processed foods. I explained how our organs work and how our hormones are affected by the foods we eat. I spoke about the issues with the North American diets and how clean eating and the "four keys to health" can revolutionize your health. After that, we covered the top five diets and who they best fit and ended with intermittent fasting. Overall, the nutritional information we have covered, I'm sure you can glean some vital information you can use on your health journey.

So where this book leaves off, the new you begins. Now, it is time for you to pick up the challenge I laid before you. I mentioned initially that "people perish because of a lack of knowledge." Now, you carry the knowledge necessary to make the changes you will need to become the healthy, fit person I know you can be. The human body is an amazing creation, capable of regenerating and healing itself when given the proper components. Use the four keys of health I laid out for you:

1. Eat fresh, local whole foods.

2. Incorporate daily exercise/movement.

3. Get proper sleep.

4. Find a way to reduce your stress.

You can do this; I believe in you. Fate led you to this book, and your determination will see you to completion. If I can do it, I know you can as well, so be strong, courageous, and willing to fight for your health!

For those who like to stay in touch or perhaps have questions, I would love to hear from you. You can find me on Instagram and Facebook at ***Keys4HealthCanada.***

Lesley Robinson

Suggested Reading and Viewing

1. **YouTube: How One Stubborn Doctor caused the Global Obesity Epidemic**

2. **YouTube: How the Sugar Industry Lobbied Harvard Scientists to Blame Saturated Fat**

3. **Book: Pure, White and Deadly** (John Yudkin)

4. **Book: The 100-mile Diet: A year of Local Eating** (Alisa Smith and J.B. Mackinnon)

5. **YouTube: Food Lies: Why We Should Be Eating More Meat, Not Less**

6. **YouTube: The Benefits of Real Milk** (by Sally Fallon at Pacific Rim College)

7. **YouTube: Top 10 Cooking Oils "The Good, Bad & Toxic! (by Dr. Sten Ekberg)**

8. **Book: Nourishing Fats....Why We Need Animal Fats for Health and Happiness (by Sally Fallon Morell)**

9. **Book: Wheat Belly** (by William Davis MD)

10. **Book: The Bitter Truth About Sugar** (by Dr. Robert Lustig)

11. Book: Metabolical... The Lure and the Lies of Processed Food (by Dr. Robert Lustig)

12. Book: Fat Chance (by Dr. Robert Lustig)

13. Book: Lies My Doctor Told Me (by Dr. Ken Berry)

14. Book: The Complete Ketogenic Diet for Beginners (by Amy Ramos)

15. The Carnivore Diet (by Dr. Shawn Baker)

16. Book: The Complete Guide to Fasting (by Nephrologist Dr. Jason Fung)

Citations

Introduction

1. Obesity and longevity. (2005). *The New-England Medical Review and Journal, 352*(24), 2555; author reply 2556– https://doi.org/10.1056/NEJM200506163522419
2. McQuillan, K., Yoshida-Montezuma, Y., Jambon, M., Vanderloo, L. M., Gonzalez, A., & Anderson, L. N. (2024). Physical activity and unexpected weight change in Ontario children and youth during the COVID-19 pandemic: A cross-sectional analysis of the Ontario Parent Survey 2. *PLoS One, 19*(2), e0292934. https://doi.org/10.1371/journal.pone.0292934

Chapter 2

1. Merriam-Webster. (n.d.). Heme. In *Merriam-Webster.com dictionary.* Retrieved from https://www.merriam-webster.com
2. Merriam-Webster. (n.d.). Non-Heme. In *Merriam-Webster.com dictionary.* Retrieved from https://www.merriam-webster.com
3. Geiker, N. R. W., Bertram, H. C., Mejborn, H., Dragsted, L. O., Kristensen, L., Carrascal, J. R., Bügel, S., & Astrup, A. (2021). Meat and human health—

Current knowledge and research gaps. *Foods, 10*(7), 1556. https://doi.org/10.3390/foods10071556

4. Moustarah, F., & Daley, S. F. (2024). Dietary Iron. In *StatPearls* [Internet]. StatPearls Publishing. Retrieved from https://www.ncbi.nlm.nih.gov/books/NBK540969/

Chapter 4

1. Centers for Disease Control and Prevention. (2015). Percentage of adults aged ≥20 years who consumed dairy* on a given day,† by amount§ and sex — National Health and Nutrition Examination Survey, United States, 2011–2012. *MMWR Weekly, 64*(27), 751.
2. Hassan, H. Y., van Erp, A., Jaeger, M., Tahir, H., Oosting, M., Joosten, L. A., & Netea, M. G. (2016). Genetic diversity of lactase persistence in East African populations. *BMC Research Notes, 9*, 8. https://doi.org/10.1186/s13104-015-1833-1

Chapter 5

1. Zion Market Research. (2022). *Metformin hydrochloride industry prospective*. Retrieved from https://www.zionmarketresearch.com/report/metformin-hydrochloride-market

2. CBC News. (2009, July 7). *Statins: The aspirin of the 21st century?* CBC News. Retrieved from https://www.cbc.ca
3. Halma, M. T. J., Tuszynski, J. A., & Marik, P. E. (2023). Cancer metabolism as a therapeutic target and review of interventions. *Nutrients, 15*(19), 4245. https://doi.org/10.3390/nu15194245

Chapter 7

1. Nishi, S. K., Viguiliouk, E., Blanco Mejia, S., Kendall, C. W. C., Bazinet, R. P., Hanley, A. J., Comelli, E. M., Salas Salvadó, J., Jenkins, D. J. A., & Sievenpiper, J. L. (2021). Are fatty nuts a weighty concern? A systematic review and meta-analysis and dose-response meta-regression of prospective cohorts and randomized controlled trials. *Obesity Reviews, 22*(11), e13330. https://doi.org/10.1111/obr.13330

Chapter 8

1. Patented Medicine Prices Review Board. (2023, May 30). *Market Intelligence Report: Antidiabetic Drugs, 2012–2021.* Ottawa, ON.
2. Yudkin, J. (2021). *Pure, white and deadly: How sugar is killing us and what we can do to stop it* (Dr. R. Lustig, Forward). Julianaszabluk.com. Retrieved from https://julianaszabluk.com

3. McKenna, M. (2016, April 7). *The sugar conspiracy.* The Guardian. Retrieved from https://www.theguardian.com/society/2016/apr/07/the-sugar-conspiracy-robert-lustig-john-yudkin
4. Rogers, K. (2023, April 5). *Eating too much 'free sugar' has 45 negative health effects*. CNN Life/Food. Retrieved from https://www.cnn.com
5. Harvard T.H. Chan School of Public Health. (2017, Spring). *Obesity rates in North America* (M. Drexler, Ed.). Harvard Public Health.
6. Harvard T.H. Chan School of Public Health. (2019, December 18). Close to half of U.S. population projected to have obesity by 2030. Harvard Public Health.
7. Statistics Canada. (2005). Adult obesity in Canada: Measured height and weight. *Catalogue 82-620-M2005001*. https://www150.statcan.gc.ca
8. NCD Risk Factor Collaboration (NCD-RisC). (2016). Worldwide trends in diabetes since 1980: A pooled analysis of 751 population-based studies with 4.4 million participants. *The Lancet, 387*(10027), 1513-1530. https://doi.org/10.1016/S0140-6736(16)00618-8
9. de la Monte, S. M., & Wands, J. R. (2008). Alzheimer's disease is type 3 diabetes—Evidence reviewed. *Journal of Diabetes Science and Technology, 2*(6), 1101–1113. https://doi.org/10.1177/193229680800200619

Chapter 9

1. Lazarus, D. (2021, September 28). *You do know that, in most cases, bottled water is just tap water?* Los Angeles Times. Retrieved from https://www.latimes.com

Chapter 10

1. U.S. Food and Drug Administration. (2022). *FDA investigation of Cronobacter infections: Powdered infant formula.* Retrieved from https://www.fda.gov
2. Dargenio, V. N., Dargenio, C., Castellaneta, S., De Giacomo, A., Laguardia, M., Schettini, F., Francavilla, R., & Cristofori, F. (2023). Intestinal barrier dysfunction and microbiota-gut-brain axis: Possible implications in the pathogenesis and treatment of autism spectrum disorder. *Nutrients, 15*(7), 1620. https://doi.org/10.3390/nu15071620
3. Reznik, E. (2024, June). *The ketogenic diet in the treatment of autism spectrum disorder* (University Electronic Theses, Dissertations & Projects). Loma Linda University.
4. Li, Q., Liang, J., Fu, N., Han, Y., & Qin, J. (2021). A ketogenic diet and the treatment of autism spectrum disorder. *Frontiers in Pediatrics, 9*, 650624. https://doi.org/10.3389/fped.2021.650624

Chapter 11

1. Sabour, H., Norouzi Javidan, A., Latifi, S., Shidfar, F., Heshmat, R., Emami Razavi, S. H., Vafa, M. R., & Larijani, B. (2015). Omega-3 fatty acids' effect on leptin and adiponectin concentrations in patients with spinal cord injury: A double-blinded randomized clinical trial. *The Journal of Spinal Cord Medicine, 38*(5), 599–606. https://doi.org/10.1179/2045772314Y.0000000251

Chapter 12

1. Mosby, I. (2013). Administering colonial science: Nutrition research and human biomedical experimentation in Aboriginal communities and residential schools, 1942–1952. *Histoire sociale/Social history, 46*, 145–172. https://doi.org/10.1353/his.2013.0015
2. Centers for Disease Control and Prevention. (2024, May 15). National diabetes statistics report. Retrieved from https://www.cdc.gov/diabetes/php/data-research/index.html
3. Mikulic, M. (2024, September 17). Market share of the leading global pharmaceutical markets 2023. *Statista*. Retrieved from https://www.statista.com

Chapter 14

1. Johns Hopkins Epilepsy Center. (n.d.). *Timeline: Ketogenic diet therapy for epilepsy.* Retrieved from https://www.hopkinsmedicine.org
2. Dowis, K., & Banga, S. (2021). The potential health benefits of the ketogenic diet: A narrative review. *Nutrients, 13*(5), 1654. https

www.ingramcontent.com/pod-product-compliance
Lightning Source LLC
Chambersburg PA
CBHW060758120626
46557CB00001B/21

9781961563629